The
HANGED MAN

The
HANGED MAN

A STORY OF MIRACLE,

MEMORY, AND

COLONIALISM IN

THE MIDDLE AGES

ROBERT BARTLETT

*Princeton
University Press
Princeton
Oxford*

Copyright © 2004 by Princeton University Press
Published by Princeton University Press,
41 William Street, Princeton, New Jersey 08540
In the United Kingdom: Princeton University Press,
3 Market Place, Woodstock, Oxfordshire OX20 1SY
All Rights Reserved.

Library of Congress Cataloging-in-Publication Data
Bartlett, Robert, 1950–
The hanged man : a story of miracle, memory, and colonialism
in the Middle Ages / Robert Bartlett.
p.   cm.
Includes bibliographical references and index.
ISBN 0-691-11719-5 (acid-free paper)
1. Hanging—Wales—History—To 1500—Case studies. 2. Executions and
executioners—Wales—History—To 1500—Case studies.
3. Near-death experiences—Religious aspects—Christianity—History of
doctrines—Middle Ages, 600–1500. 4. Resurrection—History
of doctrines—Middle Ages, 600–1500. 5. Miracles—History of
doctrines—Middle Ages, 600–1500. 6. Examination of
witnesses—Wales—History—To 1500. 7. Hanging—Wales—
History—To 1500. 8. Wales—History—1284–1536. I. Title.
HV8579.B37   2004
942.03′6—dc21   2003045783

British Library Cataloging-in-Publication Data is available.

This book has been composed in Adobe Caslon
Printed on acid-free paper. ∞
www.pupress.princeton.edu
Printed in the United States of America
1   3   5   7   9   10   8   6   4   2

In Memoriam
R. W. Southern (1912–2001)

Contents

Preface

This book takes as its starting point a dramatic event—the hanging and miraculous resurrection of a Welshman seven hundred years ago. Although the episode took place in such a distant period, we have unusually rich information about it, for no fewer than nine eyewitness accounts survive, each of them long, detailed, and vivid. The interlocking narratives of these witnesses are worth recounting for their own intrinsic interest, although it is important to understand the circumstances in which they came to be recorded, because the witnesses were giving evidence before a judicial commission and what they said was very much guided by the questions they were asked. The commission that heard the evidence about the hanging and its aftermath was concerned not with the rights and wrongs of the case but with the circumstances of the hanged man's revival: had it been the result of a miracle? This commission was a canonization inquiry, established by the pope to ascertain whether a bishop of Hereford of an earlier generation was or was not a saint. If the dead bishop had acted as a heavenly intercessor for the hanged man, this would support the claim that he was a saint; if not, not. By this point in the Middle Ages there were complex and detailed rules governing canonization, and these transactions cast much light on what people of the time considered supernatural and how they thought the supernatural could be identified.

Yet, although the issue of miracle and sanctity was the central concern of the inquiry, every part of the proceedings gave rise to new issues and new questions, which sprout strands like a tropical vine. We can try to delve deeper into what the witnesses said and what it meant. This can lead to very personal and individual questions, such as how people in the Middle Ages conceived of space and time and how their memories worked. On the other hand, using the record as a focal point, we can pan back to set it in context in the wider world of the time. This takes us to the great public events of the period—the English conquest of Wales; the trial of the Templars; or the troubles of the reign of Edward II, the first king of England to be deposed and murdered. Especially prominent is the complex world of colonial Wales, with its semi-independent Marcher lords and its long tradition of native resistance and rebellion. There is also more evidence here for the details of execution than we might wish to have.

The story involves a diverse group of people. They came from many levels of medieval society—lords and ladies, laborers, bishops and priests, rebels—and from a wide geographical range: clergymen from Gascony in southern France interrogate an English lord in London, while in Hereford a group from southern Wales is also questioned, raising some difficult translation problems for a French bishop facing the unfamiliar sound of the Welsh language. About some of this cast of characters it is possible to know a fair amount and even to infer details of their personalities and their relations with each other. For example, there seems to have been little sympathy between the highborn lady who interceded unsuccessfully for the condemned man and her stepson, who describes the corpse after the hanging in a manner that suggests gleeful satisfaction. Especially in the case of the wealthier and more powerful participants in this story, we can trace their careers both before and after their involvement in the proceedings; some of them were important figures in Church and State, diplomats, careerists, barons, and cardinals.

The story told in this book is both less and more than a reconstruction of events. It is less because it acknowledges that it is now impossible to create a complete and accurate narrative of what happened when the Welshman was hanged and revived—impossible because of gaps in our knowledge and discrepancies in the testimony. Yet it is also more than a reconstruction, for it recognizes that those gaps and discrepancies actually provide an opportunity, by showing us revealing and unusual circumstances or raising fruitful problems that cast light both on central issues and on the byways of the medieval period. The extraordinary episode of the hanging and revival of the Welshman offers a window on the wider medieval world. By analyzing the record carefully, as if with a magnifying glass, we can see details of life and thought in the Middle Ages that would otherwise not be known to us. Reading the statements that the witnesses made gives us as good an idea as we are likely to get of the spoken words of the past in the time before the tape recorder.

The
HANGED MAN

1
The Story

In the summer of 1307 an inquiry opened in London to investigate whether Thomas de Cantilupe, bishop of Hereford, who had died twenty-five years earlier, could rightly be regarded as a saint. Three commissioners, entrusted with the task by Pope Clement V, had been empowered to hear testimony about the bishop's life, the general reputation he enjoyed, and—something crucial for a favorable outcome to a canonization process—the miracles he had performed after death.

Among the first witnesses to be heard were the aristocratic lady Mary de Briouze, her stepson William de Briouze, and a chaplain of the de Briouze family, all giving evidence about the same miracle. This concerned a Welshman, William Cragh, who had been hanged for homicide on the orders of William de Briouze senior, the deceased husband of Mary de Briouze and father of William junior. It was claimed that he had been miraculously resuscitated through the intercession of Thomas de Cantilupe. This event had taken place, according to Lady Mary de Briouze, about fifteen years earlier, though she was uncertain of the exact day and month, but believed it was in winter. Her stepson was more precise: William Cragh had been captured between Michaelmas and All Saints' Day next, eighteen years ago. The chaplain offered a third dating: "The events about which he had given evidence took place sixteen years ago." Such minor vagaries of memory are not unusual; in the medieval period they would have been far more common than today, when we experience the constant hammering home of past dates by documents such as birth certificates and passports and the reiteration of current dates in newspapers and news broadcasts.

Rather than bemoan the differences among the three testimonies, we should welcome them as small indications of the different emphases and concerns of the different witnesses, pointers to the way individual perception and memory had been shaped. Perhaps it is possible to discover why Lady Mary remembered the event taking place in winter about fifteen years earlier, while her stepson pinpointed it between 29 September and 1 November eighteen years earlier, which would date it to October 1289. Discrepancy between the testimonies of different witnesses was also a central interest of the commissioners in charge of the canonization inquiry. A canonization process was a "process," that is, a trial, and the active interrogation of witnesses was part of the tradition of church courts at this time. Moreover, a detailed written record was kept of all the proceedings, so that the commissioners could easily refer back to what earlier witnesses had said. They were as likely to notice inconsistencies in testimony as the most careful historian sifting through these records.

Lady Mary's story began with a simple narrative: once, a notorious Welsh brigand, William Cragh, had been captured in her husband's lordship of Gower and had been hanged at Swansea along with another robber. He had hung on the gallows so long that everyone present judged him to be dead, and he had voided his bowels and bladder—a usual sign of death. Afterwards he had been taken down and carried off, slung across a wheel, to the chapel of Saint John the Baptist. All this, Lady Mary said, she had heard from others, for she had not seen any of it herself.

In the next part of her testimony she revealed her own personal interest in the case. Before the hanging she had asked her husband to spare the two robbers and hand them over to her. He had refused. Later, when a report was brought that the other robber was already dead, Lady Mary had asked again, requesting that she at least be given William Cragh, whom she believed to be still alive. Her husband had delayed granting her this, and eventually a report came that William Cragh was dead on the gallows; then finally her husband, in the words of the notaries jotting down her testimony, "granted him to the said lady, such as he was, and ordered him to be taken down from the gallows."

William de Briouze was from a family used to violence. His distant ancestor and namesake was one of the companions of William the Conqueror and had acquired, as part of the loot of England, the lordship of Bramber in Sussex. Later generations had added new conquests in Wales. William's great-grandfather, another namesake, had risen to dizzying heights under the patronage of King John (Gower had been one of John's gifts) but had then fallen foul of the king. This William had been dispossessed and driven into exile, while his wife and eldest son (yet another William) had been imprisoned and starved to death by the king in 1210. The family had regained its lands but their path had not been easy. Quarrels within the family had coincided with the rise of Llywelyn ap Iorwerth, one of the great Welsh leaders of the thirteenth century. In 1230 he had hanged the head of the de Briouze family, supposedly "After he had been caught in the prince's chamber with the prince's wife." Another branch managed to keep hold of Bramber and Gower. The William who hanged the Welshman William Cragh was the grandson of the de Briouze starved to death in King John's dungeons.

William de Briouze senior's son, William junior, who had succeeded him in 1291, did not regard William Cragh in the same way as did his stepmother. While she had described the Welshman as a "notorious brigand" for whom she had interceded with her husband, her stepson presented the situation differently: "Eighteen years ago between the feast of Saint Michael next and the feast of All Saints' he had been guarding the land of his father, in which there was at that time war between the Welsh and the lord Edward, the present king of England. . . . It happened at this time that a certain malefactor, who was one of the rebels against the lord king in that war, William Cragh by name, a native of Gower, was captured by the men guarding his and his father's land." Suddenly politics has made an appearance. The "notorious brigand" of Lady Mary's testimony is now a Welsh rebel against Edward I. The "war" referred to by William de Briouze junior is, in all likelihood, the rebellion of Rhys ap Mare-

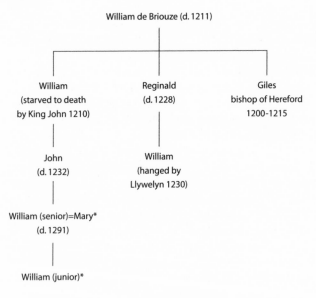

William de Briouze (d. 1211)

William	Reginald	Giles
(starved to death by King John 1210)	(d. 1228)	bishop of Hereford 1200-1215
John (d. 1232)	William (hanged by Llywelyn 1230)	
William (senior)=Mary* (d. 1291)		
William (junior)*		

*the witnesses in the canonization process of 1307

Fig. 1 Simplified family tree of the de Briouze family in the thirteenth century.

dudd, a descendant of the ancient line of the princes of Deheubarth (southwest Wales) and lord of the land of Ystrad Tywi, which bordered Gower to the north. He had been an active collaborator of the English king, Edward I, during the final annexation of Wales in 1282–83, but had found the postwar settlement not to his liking. In the summer of 1287 he went into rebellion and, although his lands were occupied by Edward's vastly superior forces and the rebellion was virtually crushed by January 1288, Rhys ap Maredudd was not captured until the spring of 1292, when he was betrayed and executed. William de Briouze junior seems to have been referring to that period when the revolt was no longer a threat but its leader was still at large.

The testimony of William de Briouze junior to the papal commissioners in the canonization process adds considerable detail to the account of the hanging. He named the other Welshman hanged alongside William Cragh as "another malefactor" called Trahaearn ap Hywel. The two men were hanged early in the morning on the gallows "about half an English league" from the de Briouze castle at Swansea. In the early afternoon, after the household had eaten, a report came that the central beam of the gallows had collapsed. The gallows were obviously visible from the castle because William de Briouze senior, his son, and many of his household were able to look out from the hall of the castle and see this. The two hanged men had fallen to the ground, but both were reported to be already dead. William de Briouze commanded that Trahaearn be buried but William Cragh, "because he was a very famous and public malefactor," was strung up again and hung on the gallows until sunset.

The personal animus felt by the lord of Gower toward William Cragh is mentioned on other occasions. One of the standard questions that commissioners in canonization proceedings asked was whether an apparent miracle could have been effected either by trickery or by natural causes. In the case of a hanged man surviving, it was obvious to wonder whether deception, bribery, or connivance might have been involved. When this was put to him, William de Briouze junior was adamant. He thought this possibility could be ruled out "since his father and he himself and their officials and servants hated William Cragh because he was the worst of malefactors and he had perpetrated many wicked deeds in their land, killing men and robbing and burning, and he was a man of great strength." The point was reiterated by the chaplain, William of Codineston, who also thought fraud or deceit impossible, "because the lord de Briouze and his justices, officials, and servants hated William Cragh very much and rejoiced greatly at his hanging and death and the servants and justices were present at the hanging."

Even if the collaboration of the executioners could be dismissed as a possibility, it was still vital to establish that William Cragh had in fact been dead—it was no miracle to revive a living man. Lady Mary had mentioned the fact that he had voided his bowels and bladder but this was hearsay, not firsthand evidence. Nor could the chaplain, William of Codineston, offer a firsthand account, "for he had not wished to follow the malefactors when they were led out of the town of Swansea to be hanged, on account of his priestly office." He had heard, however, that William Cragh was still breathing when the gallows had collapsed. After he had been strung up again and hung for a while, the rope had broken. The two hanged men had then been carried to the chapel of Saint John, though whether on a wheel, as Lady Mary had said, the chaplain did not know. However, he had heard that some people had said that while Trahaearn's body was cold, William Cragh's was still warm, although others considered him dead.

The most vivid account, if that is the right word, of William Cragh's body after the hanging comes from William de Briouze junior. He had seen the hanging only from a distance, but after William Cragh's friends and kinsfolk had, "through his father's grace," carried him off—he did not know whether on a wheel or by some other method—to the house of a burgess of Swansea—whose name he did not remember—the young lord went down from the castle with some companions to see the corpse. He must have found it a gratifying sight. The body lay within the house by the main door, stretched out on the ground "in the way that a dead man lies." The passage of eighteen years (if that span is correct) had not dimmed the image:

> His whole face was black and in parts bloody or stained with blood. His eyes had come out of their sockets and hung outside the eyelids and the sockets were filled with blood. His mouth, neck, and throat and the parts around them, and also his nostrils, were filled with blood, so that it was impossible in the natural course of things for him to breathe air through his nostrils or through his mouth or through his throat . . . his tongue hung out of his mouth, the length of a man's finger, and it was completely black and swollen and as thick with the blood sticking to it that it seemed the size of a man's two fists together.

Having viewed William Cragh's body in this state, William de Briouze returned to the castle and told his stepmother, the Lady Mary, about what he had seen. She responded with compassion:

"This man has been hanged twice and has suffered a great penalty. Let us pray to God and Saint Thomas de Cantilupe that he give him life and, if he give him life, we will conduct him to Saint Thomas," meaning by this that he would be taken to Thomas de Cantilupe's tomb in Hereford Cathedral to give thanks. William de Briouze reported his stepmother's words literally in the vernacular French used by the upper class of the time (*Prium deu et seint Thomas de Cantelup qe luy donne vie et si il luy donne vie, nous le amenerons a lavant dit seint Thomas*). Lady Mary was clearly persevering in her attempt to save William Cragh's life, despite the obstinacy of her husband and the seeming hopelessness of the situation. Her own testimony agrees with that of her stepson: "She had frequently heard tell before this that God worked miracles through Saint Thomas de Cantilupe, to whom the lady said she had a special devotion; along with her ladies-in-waiting and also with the men who were there at the time, with devotion and on bended knee, she asked Saint Thomas de Cantilupe to ask God to restore life to William who had been hanged." They added the Lord's Prayer and the Ave Maria.

This invocation of the saint was a crucial step in the transformation of an amazing escape from death into a miracle. If the witnesses had simply established that William Cragh had been restored to life, the mechanism and, more important, the meaning of the event would have been left obscure. Lady Mary's appeal to a specific, named saint, to whom she had a special devotion, and whose reputation for miracle working was already established, was one act, among others to be discussed shortly, that made it possible to construe William Cragh's escape from death by hanging as a miracle of Thomas de Cantilupe and hence a piece of evidence supporting the case that he was a saint. Sentence had been passed long ago on the Welsh "malefactor"; a verdict was yet to be given on Thomas de Cantilupe.

By the year 1307 (during which the hearings took place) the inquisitorial technique of the church courts had become meticulous, searching, and often pedantic. We have already seen how Lady Mary's introduction of the wheel on which William Cragh was supposedly carried from the gallows meant that both

William de Briouze junior and the chaplain William of Codineston had to answer questions about this, perhaps with some bemusement. Lady Mary's invocation of Thomas de Cantilupe was likewise subject to intense scrutiny. When she uttered her prayer, the commissioners wanted to know, did she believe and have faith and hope that God would, through the merits of Saint Thomas, hear her prayer? Lady Mary replied, perhaps rather sharply, yes, because otherwise she would not have asked.

She answered in a similar vein that those who prayed with her believed that their prayers would be answered and that, at the time they uttered those prayers, they believed that William Cragh was truly dead. Asked the names of those who prayed with her, she said that one of them was a lady-in-waiting of hers called Elena de la Chambre, from the diocese of Saint Davids (in which Swansea was situated) but she could not remember the names of the others present. The invocation had taken place in Lady Mary's chamber in the castle of Swansea.

The distinction between the lady's chamber, where she waited with her ladies for news from outside, and the hall, from which William de Briouze senior and junior could see the gallows, emerges clearly from these narratives. Perhaps more striking is Lady Mary's inability to remember the names of her ladies-in-waiting (although, as we shall see, she could recall more than just Elena) or other retainers. It would be premature to attribute this to a high turnover among attendants, individual forgetfulness, or haughty disdain for those more lowly than herself—all explanations that spring to mind.

Lady Mary's next step brings us to one of the more remarkable practices involved in the veneration of the saints in the medieval period: "measuring to the saint." When the help of a saint was sought on behalf of victims of sickness or calamity, a thread or cord might be taken and used to measure the length (and sometimes also the breadth) of the body. The "measuring" implied a promise that, if there were a miraculous cure, a candle the length of the cord or thread used would be made for the saint. The ailing individual would be measured "to" a particular saint, thus entrusting him or her to the saint's care.

This is exactly the practice that Lady Mary employed in the aftermath of her prayer to Thomas de Cantilupe. She sent a lady-in-waiting—not Elena de la Chambre but Sunehild,[4] thus another named attendant—"to measure William according to the English custom" (the implication of these words is that the Welsh did things differently). Sunehild returned, reporting that she had done so. Lady Mary did not know whether Sunehild was still alive nor where she might be but her stepson was better informed; he knew that the lady was "now dead." Moreover, he added that as well as measuring William Cragh "to Saint Thomas," she had also "bent a silver penny over his head according to the custom of England," this being another distinctive way of making a vow to a saint and entrusting someone to him or her.

That the case of William Cragh had thus been put in the hands of Saint Thomas de Cantilupe was as clear as possible: through explicit invocation, through measuring to the saint, through bending a votive penny. It was now the saint's turn to act. He did not disappoint his devotees: "After he had been measured, William Cragh remained in the same state until around the middle of the night, and then began to breathe in and out and to move a leg" (according to the testimony of William de Briouze); "After he had been measured, not immediately but after an hour or so, William moved his tongue a little and after another space of time moved a foot and afterwards gradually began to recover strength in his limbs" (according to the testimony of the chaplain William of Codineston).

All witnesses agreed that the hanged man's recovery was gradual. The chaplain said William Cragh was infirm for "eight or ten days." William de Briouze junior visited him in the burgess's house in Swansea on the fourth day after his recovery and found him lying in bed, with much improvement in the state of his tongue, eyes, and throat, but still unable to speak or see. For some time the convalescent could not swallow solid food but only soup and broth, which Lady Mary prepared for him in her quarters in Swansea Castle.

At this point we can introduce some evidence from a new voice, that of William Cragh himself; for although both William de Briouze and the chaplain reported at the hearings in 1307 that he had died two or three years earlier, the Welshman's statements at the time of the hanging were recounted by all three witnesses— Lady Mary, her step-son, and the chaplain. So far William Cragh has been encountered as a "notorious brigand," in the words of Lady Mary and the chaplain, or, as William de Briouze put it, a Welsh rebel, or through his prolonged and grotesque physical sufferings on the gallows. Now it is possible to hear, if only at second hand, his views on the situation.

Perhaps most instructive is the picture painted by the chaplain, William of Codineston. He tells how William Cragh, after he had recovered his health, came before Lord William de Briouze senior and Lady Mary his wife in the chamber of the castle of Swansea (the chaplain William himself being present) and there explained that, while he was being led to the gallows, he had prayed to Saint Thomas de Cantilupe to intercede with God to save him from hanging. He said all this, reported the chaplain, "with great fear and apprehension, for he wondered whether he would be hanged again."

He need not have worried. Cragh's invocation of Thomas de Cantilupe, to whom Lady Mary, as we have heard, had a special devotion, was effective enough to defuse, or at least silence, the deep hatred that William de Briouze felt towards the Welshman. William Cragh's story, as reported by all three witnesses, actually involved something more elaborate than the simple invocation of Saint Thomas de Cantilupe on his way to the gallows, for he also claimed that, while he was hanging, there appeared a bishop, clad in white garments, who helped him, either by supporting his feet (as Lady Mary and the chaplain reported) or by replacing his tongue in his mouth (as William de Briouze junior said). What is most remarkable about these reports is that all agreed that William Cragh did not himself claim that the visionary bishop who helped him on the gallows was Thomas de Cantilupe. If this is true, it is possible that the story of his invocation of the saint on the way to be hanged is a retrospective invention, and that Thomas de Cantilupe's first intervention in these events was, in fact, when Lady Mary first thought of invoking him. William

Cragh did, after all, have very good reasons for accepting the interpretation of his remarkable survival as a miracle of Saint Thomas. He had no wish to face William de Briouze's justice yet again.

Every miracle story must end with proper thanks to the saint responsible. Once it had been generally accepted that William Cragh's remarkable survival was to be understood as a miracle of Thomas de Cantilupe, a journey to the saint's tomb in Hereford Cathedral was a necessity. William de Briouze senior went, with what emotions we do not know; his wife Lady Mary went, presumably with complex feelings of satisfaction; and William de Briouze junior went, all on horseback; while William Cragh, the noose from the gallows around his neck, accompanied them on foot. It took three days to reach Hereford and when they arrived the canons of the cathedral were informed of the miracle. Bells were rung, the *Te Deum* sung, and William de Briouze senior commissioned a wax model of a man hanging from a gallows, which, along with William Cragh's noose, was presented at the saint's tomb. In a final submissive gesture, William Cragh promised to go off to the Holy Land. "After that," testified Lady Mary, "she did not see him." William de Briouze junior and the chaplain had a different story; yes, he had vowed to go to the Holy Land but had in fact returned to Wales. William de Briouze junior reported that "he saw him afterwards in his land for ten years or more on many occasions and finally William Cragh died in his land of natural causes about two years ago."

2
The Questioners

I t may be that Mary de Briouze, William de Briouze junior, and their chaplain were garrulous types, given to long-winded and circumstantial narratives at the slightest invitation. It is certainly the case that they were subject to the most sophisticated inquisitorial procedure that Europe had yet produced. The public and academic culture of the Church in the later Middle Ages was based on a ruthlessly interrogatory style—"when, why, with whom, with what bystanders?" Inquests into heresy, theological inquiries, and, likewise, canonization processes all involved careful and structured interrogation, which was shaped both by the "inquisitorial model" (the form that had been established) and by the individuals into whose hands it was placed.

Both Roman Law, as developed in ancient Rome and transmitted to the Middle Ages, and the law of the Church (canon law) that had grown from it presumed that the judge or judges would dominate the court, actively interrogating parties, specifying procedures, and passing sentences. This picture is very different from that of the Anglo-American jury trial, where the judge presides but interrogation is in the hands of specialist lawyers and the verdict the preserve of a committee of lay people. It was the "Romano-canonical" system that lay behind the canonization process of Thomas de Cantilupe. The judges expected to be able to quiz the witnesses and they did so according to a detailed and lengthy questionnaire. This meant, of course, that the initial decisions regarding the content of this questionnaire would shape the witnesses' responses and, hence, the story itself, just as in a scientific experiment the outcome is shaped by the initial hypothesis and choice of method.

The Romano-canonical inquisitorial method developed its sophisticated form in the 150 years before the Cantilupe canonization process. It evolved in an intellectual environment ("scholasticism") that relied extensively on a "question and answer" method and on analytic technique, resolving questions and issues into their constituent parts or varying senses, and in a political environment (the perceived threat of heresy) that encouraged vigorous interrogation, thorough examination—including torture in some cases—and careful recording and sifting of evidence.

The impact of this method is evident in many areas of public life in Catholic Europe but most relevant here is, naturally, its part in shaping canonization procedure. Until the twelfth century the decision that someone could be regarded as a saint was not the special prerogative of the pope—he could indeed declare someone a saint, but then, so could any bishop. Usually some form of inquiry would be made into the life of the candidate for canonization, and especially into the miracles that he or she had performed after death, but such inquiries were not subject to strict formal rules of procedure and were almost invariably left to the parties seeking the canonization. It was the monks of Canterbury, for instance, who drew up the huge record of the miracles of their archbishop, Thomas Becket, canonized by the pope in 1173.

Around the year 1200, under the strong hand of Pope Innocent III (himself a renowned canon lawyer) the canonization process was given a firmer and more clearly legal shape. Once a preliminary examination had revealed a prima facie case, the pope would appoint commissioners with power to hear witnesses on the life and miracles of a potential saint. The witnesses would swear an oath to the truth of the testimony, and their names and other details would be noted. The record of the proceedings would then be sent to the pope, who would make a decision in consultation with the cardinals. The power to canonize, in this full and public sense, was declared to be a prerogative of the pope alone.

One of the earliest surviving dossiers of documents concerning a papal canonization is that of Gilbert of Sempringham, founder of the only medieval monastic order to originate in England, who died in 1189 and was canonized by Innocent III in 1202. This dossier contains a "Life of Gilbert," a collection of letters relating both to events during Gilbert's lifetime and to the canonization process itself and two collections of miracles—one of which records the results of an enquiry by a papal commission of three, just as in Cantilupe's case, although the witnesses in Gilbert's case do not seem to have been questioned according to the articles of a questionnaire. The earliest surviving example of a set of questions used to shape a canonization process, is the one employed in the inquest into the life and miracles of Saint Dominic that took place in Bologna and southern France in 1233, twelve years after Dominic's death. In the following year the publication of the first papally authorized code of canon law, the Decretals, reemphasized the papal monopoly of canonization: "You may not revere anyone as a saint without the permission of the Roman Church."

By the middle of the thirteenth century the procedure involved in a canonization process had been clearly defined; however, it was complex, expensive, and usually lengthy. Traveling to Rome with requests, summoning witnesses, recording the proceedings, and winning the cardinals' favour could all be arduous. Even in a case with as much political weight behind it as that of Louis IX of France it was twelve years between Louis's death in 1270 and the inquest into his life and miracles in 1282, and another fifteen before he officially became "Saint Louis" in 1297. About half of all canonization processes in the Middle Ages simply became bogged down in the sand of cost, chance, and politics, and never reached an outcome.

Thomas de Cantilupe's case, seen in this context, made fairly satisfactory progress. The bishop died in 1282 and (as we will see in more detail later, in chapter 11) miracles at his tomb began in 1287. This prompted an intermittent but tenacious campaign, initiated by the bishop and chapter of Hereford but with the backing of many English bishops and of the king, Edward I, to have Cantilupe's sanctity recognized. Eventually, twenty-four years after the bishop's death, Pope Clement V responded by ordering the official enquiry.

The papal letter appointing three commissioners to investigate the case was issued at Bordeaux on 23 August 1306 (the original letter, twenty-three inches wide and eighteen inches high, but now lacking its seal or "bull," survives today in Hereford Cathedral Library). The place of issue is not surprising. Clement V was a Gascon by birth and was soon to move the papal headquarters from Rome to Avignon, in the south of France, beginning that phase of papal history known, neutrally, as "the Avignon Papacy" or, in a more hostile formulation, as "the Babylonian Captivity." As a Gascon, the pope was born a subject not only of the king of France but also of the king of England, who in this period was also duke of Gascony, under the French Crown. Perhaps this helps explain Clement's willingness to open the canonization proceedings, which had been requested by Edward I, among others.

In the letter the pope explains that "happy rumors" had been brought to him by representatives of the dean and chapter of Hereford, suggesting that not only had their late bishop, Thomas de Cantilupe, lived a life of exemplary virtue, but now God had begun to perform miracles through his merits at his tomb in Hereford Cathedral: "We have heard that the blind recover their sight there, the lame walk, and the dead rise again." The Hereford delegation had been backed up by the bishop of Worcester, William of Gainsborough, who had spent the entire winter of 1305–6 with the pope, involved in negotiations concerning the crusade and peace between England and France. He was a famous Franciscan theologian, familiar at the papal court and convinced of Cantilupe's sanctity. "We firmly believe," he wrote, "that Lord Thomas in his day pleased the Lord as a high priest and hence he was and is without a doubt to be numbered among the saints."

In response to the urgings of the Hereford representatives and the bishop of Worcester, Pope Clement had asked three cardinals at the papal court to undertake a search of the archives for relevant material; these had turned up letters of King Edward, the archbishop of York, fifteen bishops, seven abbots, eleven earls, and many English barons and nobles attesting to the sanctity of Cantilupe's life and the fact of the miracles. In light of this Clement commanded his three commissioners to "inquire most diligently into the truth concerning the faith, morals, and life of this bishop of Hereford and into his reputation and the miracles and other things pertaining to the business, both by witnesses whom the dean and chapter will produce and in other ways." He gave them four months to do the job.

It is time to turn to the three high ecclesiastics, important men in their day, entrusted with the task:

> William Durand, bishop of Mende;
> Ralph Baldock, bishop of London;
> William de Testa, archdeacon of Aran in the diocese of Comminges.

William Durand, bishop of Mende in the south of France, was a member of a family that had produced one of the outstanding ecclesiastics of the thirteenth century—his uncle and namesake, William Durand the elder, who was also his predecessor as bishop of Mende (1285–96). William Durand the elder was known as "the Speculator," not because of his reflective turn of mind but because he had written the *Speculum Iudiciale* ("Judicial Mirror"), the standard guide to Romano-canonical procedure. When William Durand the younger faced issues of procedure in ecclesiastical courts, he had the comfort of knowing that his uncle had literally written the book on the subject. Trained at Bologna, the great center of legal studies, and with enormous experience as both a judge in the papal court and a governor in the Papal State that straddled Italy, William Durand the elder had also written major works on canon law and liturgy.

William Durand the younger stepped into his uncle's shoes. Appointed bishop of Mende in 1296 as his successor, apparently while quite young, he was commissioned by Clement V to tour the Papal States from 1305 to 1306, establishing peace, if possible, in these disjointed and unruly territories—rule from a distance was difficult. A native of the south of France, Clement V spent most of his early years as pope there and, in 1309, as already mentioned, was to establish the papacy permanently at Avignon, far from Rome. A commission like that of William Durand and his fellow-commissioner, Pilifort, abbot of Lombez (an abbey in the diocese of Toulouse), involving the "pacifying and reforming" of central Italy, provided a distant finger of the pope. They did their best, negotiating with local communities and issuing rules, perhaps without much hope that they would be followed, and acting as mediators between warring factions. In one especially creative settlement the men of the commune of Camerino in the Marche were ordered to make peace with the surrounding communities of San Severino, Fabriano, and Metelica: each side was to give up the banners and flags it had captured from the opposition; and sixty-eight women from Camerino, "some of the upper class, some of the middle class, and some from the rest" were to be married to men of the surrounding villages and sixty-eight men from the surrounding villages were to be married to women of Camerino. The outcome of this piece of social engineering is unknown.

The bishop of Mende was not only the spiritual father of his flock but also himself a great territorial lord, possessed of an unusual degree of political and judicial authority in his diocese. As such, William Durand was as familiar with castles, jails, and gallows as was William de Briouze. In fact, immediately before coming to England to begin the inquest into Thomas de Cantilupe, Durand had concluded an important power-sharing agreement with Philip IV, king of France, on the government of his diocese and this was symbolized by the erection of a gallows with one foot in the king's land and the other in the bishop's. He seems to have had some aptitude for steering a course between his two great masters, the pope and the king of France, even during years of conflict, such as those that marked the clash between King Philip and Pope Boniface VIII, who was virtually hounded to death by the French king in 1303. The local aristocracy of Mende proved more intractable. They regarded the negotiations between bishop and king as particularly threatening to their position and, in 1304, a group of them conspired to assassinate Durand; they failed and, with royal officers and forces also bearing down on them, were crushed. William Durand the younger had surely already faced more difficult situations when he came upon the case of the Welshman hanged in Swansea.

Ralph Baldock's career had been less dramatic than Durand's. He warranted the title "Master," which meant he must have studied at university, and had worked his way up the ecclesiastical ladder of the diocese of London, becoming a canon of Saint Paul's, archdeacon of Middlesex in 1278, and dean in 1294. When entrusted with the task of deciding whether Thomas de Cantilupe was a saint, Ralph Baldock had only recently been enthroned as bishop of London. Although he had been elected bishop on 24 February 1304, wrangling among the canons of London had led to a dispute that was settled only after an appeal to the pope himself. In September 1304 the bishop-elect had set off overseas to pursue his case. It was a difficult time, with the papacy vacant, but the opponents of his election withdrew their objections and eventually, in a letter from Lyons on 1 February 1306, the new pope, Clement V, confirmed Ralph's election and ordered Peter, cardinal-bishop of Sabina, to consecrate him. On 17 July of that year, almost two and a half years after his election, Ralph Baldock was enthroned in Saint Paul's as bishop of London.

Even in the short time between taking up his diocese and receiving the papal command to inquire into Cantilupe's sanctity the new bishop had encountered the problem of policing the supernatural. An image in the church at Ashingdon in Essex had acquired a popular reputation for miraculous powers. "An innumerable crowd of people flocks to the church," Bishop Baldock noted, but he was troubled by their "easy belief" in these miracles. In September 1306 he instructed two of his more learned clergy to conduct an investigation: inspect the image in person, convoke the local priests and respectable laymen, and find out "through whom and how the miracles were first publicized and what was the cause of the sudden confluence of people." Until they had come to a satisfactory conclusion they should impound the offerings that had been made to the image. The bishop was concerned that people "should not be deceived by vain illusions or false teachings, as we have learned has happened in many places, occasioned by the illicit desire for profit." He was clearly well prepared, by temperament and training, to serve on Cantilupe's canonization process. He would know how to ask "through whom and how and what was the cause?"

In the spring of 1307, as the proceedings about Cantilupe were imminent, Ralph Baldock added high office in the kingdom to his ecclesiastical position. He was clearly already a trusted servant of the king, for he had been sworn in as a member of the royal council at the parliament of Carlisle in January 1307. Edward I's chancellor died on 19 April 1307 at Fountains Abbey in Yorkshire and the aged monarch commanded that the royal seal, which it was the chancellor's task to guard and use, be taken to Westminster and entrusted to his new chancellor, the bishop of London. This was done and by 3 May Baldock was sealing writs with the seal at his manor house in Stepney. It is not quite clear why Edward chose him. Possibly it was his performance as a tax collector, for in 1300–1302 while dean of Saint Paul's, and again in the twelve months before his appointment as chancellor, he had been responsible for levying the 10 percent income tax that the pope had imposed on the English Church on the understanding that pope and king would share the proceeds. By far the larger share of these taxes went to the king, and perhaps Edward had been impressed by the way Bishop Ralph procured funds for his endless wars. In any event, the commissioners now included one of the highest ministers of the kingdom, for the chancellor was in charge of the royal secretariat and responsible for the issue of the letters and writs that conveyed the commands and grants of the king. Thomas de Cantilupe had himself served briefly as chancellor in the tumultuous year 1265, when Simon de Montfort and his supporters sought to control and check the government of Edward I's father, Henry III. A successor in the office was now about to decide the case for his sanctity.

William de Testa was, like Pope Clement V, a Gascon, from the town of Condom (its name is only accidentally that of a form of birth control) and had first come to the attention of the future pope when he was bishop of Comminges and William was the archdeacon of Aran in that same diocese. The diocese of Saint-

Bertrand-de-Comminges straddled the Pyrenees (and in these very years Aran was the subject of dispute between the kings of Aragon and the kings of France) but was certainly part of Gascony, where Clement V was born. A few months after his election as pope in the summer of 1305, Clement sent William de Testa, described as "his chaplain," along with another southern French ecclesiastic, Raymond, bishop of Lescar, on an embassy to England, concerned primarily with establishing peace between the kings of England and France. The letter informing Edward I of this commission is dated one year earlier, almost to the day, than the bull instituting the commission to enquire into the sanctity of Thomas de Cantilupe. Papal commissioners were busy with many tasks.

William de Testa's main job, however, was raising money for the pope. On 1 February 1306 he was charged by Clement V with collecting an entirely new form of papal taxation, annates; that is, the first year's income from a church benefice after it had become vacant. Henceforth, when a rector or canon or other clergyman died, the pope, not the next rector or canon, would have the first year's income from the post. This innovation was understandably unpopular. Edward I appears to have been willing to allow it in return for a series of favors the new pope had done for him: granting the king the whole income from the 10 percent income tax on the clergy; suspending the archbishop of Canterbury, against whom the king had a grudge; and absolving him from the oaths he had been forced to take in 1297 to observe certain rights of his subjects. On 23 March 1306, seven weeks after being appointed collector of annates, William de Testa was made collector general for papal taxes within the British Isles. Both he and Ralph Baldock of London were thus seasoned financial administrators when they undertook the canonization process.

It is clear that when he chose the commissioners to investigate the sanctity of Thomas de Cantilupe, Pope Clement did not look for especially holy men but for experienced papal administrators, and exhibited a clear preference for those from the south of France. As far as is known, neither Testa nor Durand had visited England before the pope sent them there in 1305 and 1307 respectively. He did know them and their work well, however; he had been Testa's superior as bishop of Comminges and had entrusted Durand with the hard task of pacifying the Papal States. Ralph Baldock must also have been known to him personally from his visit to the papal court during the dispute over Baldock's election. All three commissioners were university trained, probably in law. Their experience of law, administration, and tax collecting did not debar them from deciding who was a saint, but in fact qualified them to do it.

The Plot Thickens

One or two complications needed to be dealt with before the commissioners could begin their task. First, it had been pointed out to the pope that Thomas de Cantilupe had actually been in a state of excommunication when he died. An excommunicate was cast out of the body of the Church for some offence and could only be reconciled and rejoin the community of the faithful after the sentence of excommunication had been lifted. Thomas's excommunication had been imposed by John Pecham, archbishop of Canterbury (1279–92), during a dispute between the two prelates about their relative jurisdiction within the diocese of Hereford. Thomas had, in fact, died in Italy while pursuing this issue at the papal court. Consequently, nine days after he had issued the letter commanding the inquiry into Cantilupe's sanctity, Clement V issued another, instructing the same commissioners first to conduct an investigation into whether Cantilupe had died excommunicate. If so, the inquiry into his sanctity need not take place—there was no room for an excommunicate saint.

The inquiry into Cantilupe's excommunication commenced on 20 April 1307 in the chapter-house of Ralph Baldock's cathedral in London. William Durand had been in England since 22 February. William de Testa, delayed at Carlisle where the English parliament had been meeting, had been afraid that he might not be able to attend. The choice of this unusual site for parliament is explained by the virtual removal of the English government to the north of England in the last year of Edward's reign, as he attempted to crush Robert Bruce, who had been crowned king of Scots, in defiance of Edward, on 25 March 1306. The aged English king, known as the "Hammer of the Scots," had gone north in the summer of 1306, never to return. He spent five months lying sick in the monastery of Lanercost, near Carlisle, to which city he summoned parliament. The parliament actually spent less time in discussing the war with Robert Bruce than in attacking William de Testa for the papal taxes he was seeking to levy. It condemned the "various new and intolerable burdens, oppressions, wrongs, and extortions" for which the papal nuncio was responsible. On 20 March, Testa wrote to the bishops of Mende and London from Carlisle, explaining that he was busy with the affairs of the Roman Church and could not participate in the investigation into Cantilupe's excommunication. He was too pessimistic, however, and was in fact present for the first hearings, exactly a month later, in the chapter-house of Saint Paul's cathedral.

The commissioners heard forty-four witnesses, examined various letters, and took the advice of Peter, cardinal-bishop of Sabina (the same man who had consecrated the bishop of London the previous year), who was in London with his learned entourage not only to finalize arrangements for the marriage of Edward, Prince of Wales, and Isabella, daughter of the king of France, but also, according to one hostile English monk, "to fleece the English churches." On 30 June 1307 this inquest into Cantilupe's excommunication came to an end, with the commissioners deciding that it had turned up nothing that should prevent their undertaking the other inquiry into Thomas's case for sanctity. Thomas may have been excommunicated by his hostile archbishop, but he had been absolved in Italy before his death.

Finally, on 13 July 1307, at the prompting of Henry of Schorne, archdeacon of Hereford and representative of the dean and chapter of Hereford in the case, the commissioners agreed to open the canonization process. Edward I had died six days earlier leading his troops toward Scotland, but this did not prevent the commissioners going about their business. They drafted the oath to be sworn by the witnesses, they heard the oaths of Henry of

Schorne and the notaries whose task it was to make a written record of the proceedings, they drew up a list of twenty-five articles that formed the questionnaire that would shape the questions they asked of the witnesses. These articles were grouped into three sections, each of which might prove elaborate: "faith, life, and character"; "reputation, public report, and opinion"; "miracles." Article 5, for example, asked "if he [Thomas] was by nature discreet and prudent, humble, gentle and mild, patient and benevolent, sober, modest and chaste; if he was diligent in prayer, devotion, and contemplation or meditation; if he was just, God-fearing, and merciful and peaceable; if he suffered persecution or adversity in his life, and of what type and for what cause."

On the day following the drafting of these meticulous questions, 14 July 1307, the commissioners heard the first witnesses, including Lady Mary de Briouze, and on the following day her stepson and the de Briouze chaplain. Their evidence on the miraculous resurrection of William Cragh, our starting point, was only part of a chorus of testimony, some on Cantilupe's other miracles, some on his admirable life, the merit of which was exemplified by a harsh regime towards his own body, an unbending defence of the rights of his church, and an outspoken anti-Semitism. Not only had Bishop Thomas opposed the promotion of Jewish converts to positions of authority, he had argued that the remaining Jews ("enemies of God and rebels against the faith") should either convert or be expelled from the kingdom. Thomas de Cantilupe died in 1282, so he did not live to see the enforcement of this policy in 1290, when Edward I expelled all Jews from his kingdom, but there is no doubt he would have been gratified by it.

After hearing dozens of witnesses in London, the commission recognized that it might make sense to continue the hearings in Hereford, since so many of those summoned to give evidence were local people. Accordingly, on 28 August 1307 the entourage took up its task in Saint Katherine's chapel, a remarkable two story Romanesque building that had been built by the first Norman bishop of Hereford and was situated adjacent to the cathedral. In this capacious building—its central space was over forty feet square—they worked their way slowly through much more testimony. Summer turned to autumn and then the first hints of winter appeared. On 6 November the representative of the Hereford cathedral chapter produced six witnesses (numbered 148 through 153 in the record) to prove that William Cragh had been restored to life after hanging through the merits of Saint Thomas de Cantilupe. The first of the six was William Cragh himself, despite William de Briouze's July testimony that Cragh had died a few years ago. Obviously the three de Briouze witnesses were imprecise not only on matters of chronology. William Cragh had risen from the dead once again.

The first issue that confronted the commissioners when dealing with William Cragh was that he spoke only Welsh. There had been no major problems dealing with the first 147 witnesses, who deposed in Latin (mainly clergy), French (the upper class), or English (everybody else), but this Welsh speaker presented a greater difficulty. William Cragh's Welsh monolingualism had indeed been noted earlier, in the testimony of William of Codineston, the de Briouze chaplain. According to him, William Cragh, while on his way to the gallows, had shown manifest signs that he wished to confess his sins, but this had not been possible with the chaplain "because William Cragh could not speak English and the witness [William of Codineston], who is English, could not speak or understand Welsh." The condemned man thus confessed to another priest, whose name William of Codineston could not remember when asked by the commissioners of 1307.

Whatever language a witness employed, the testimony would be rendered into standard ecclesiastical Latin by the notaries. They, as well as the commissioners, included both Frenchmen and Englishmen (see the discussion in chapter 10). So far they had managed well but the arrival of William Cragh, the hanged man, prompted further improvisation; the solution was to conscript two Franciscan friars from the convent at Hereford. The first was called (in English form) John Young or (in Welsh) Sion Ieuanc and the second, Maurice of Pencoyd; they "were said to come from Wales and to understand and be able to speak the Welsh language." The choice of Franciscans is significant. The

Order, which had begun a century earlier, inspired by Saint Francis and encouraged by Pope Innocent III, was truly international, with convents from Palestine to Ireland and from Portugal to the Baltic Sea, and it took preaching seriously. To reach a wide lay audience the friars needed to master the everyday languages of every region where they were active. Hence the choice of two Welsh-speaking friars, from the English convent of Hereford, to translate the Welsh of William Cragh into a Latin that the southern-French-speaking bishop of Mende and archdeacon of Aran would understand, made good sense.

William Cragh then came forward. Or, as the record describes him, "William ap Rhys of the parish of Swansea in the diocese of Saint Davids, whom some call William Cragh, that is 'the Scabby.'" With the two friars as interpreters, he was read the articles of interrogation, swore the oath, and gave his personal details. He said that he was a free man, was not absolutely certain of his age but thought he was about forty-five, and lived under the lordship of the baron William de Briouze, who (the recorders noted) "was examined earlier among the first witnesses about this miracle, along with his stepmother and chaplain." Not at this preliminary stage but on a later day he told the commissioners that he was the son of Rhys ap Gwilym by his wife Swanith of the parish of Llanrhidian. Most significantly, he stated that "he is a poor man, living with his kinsfolk, because his land was taken away from him by his lord."

Asked to describe the circumstances of his hanging, William explained that his lord had accused him of killing thirteen men and had imprisoned him in the castle of Swansea. Held for fifteen days and questioned by William de Briouze, William Cragh denied his guilt but was nevertheless taken out to be hanged "on the Monday after Michaelmas next, fifteen years ago." He was led by his own relatives, Gruffudd Foel, Dafydd ap Gruffudd, and Ithel Fychan, to the gallows on a high hill near the castle, and he had to carry with him for his own execution "a rope thicker than the knot that the Franciscans usually have on their belts." With every word mediated via two Franciscan friars, the image was particularly expressive. Immediately after he himself was hanged, William Cragh continued, Trahaearn ap Hywel, who had been led to the gallows by his side, was also strung up. William's last conscious sensation as he dangled on the gallows was the roar of the crowd when Trahaearn was hanged. William Cragh's testimony concerning events after his loss of consciousness was obviously not first-hand, but hearsay. "As he heard tell," Trahaearn had died immediately, then the gallows had broken and both men had fallen to the ground. He had felt nothing at this time, nor when he was again hanged. Nor did he know how long any of this had taken.

Here the commissioners concluded their day's proceedings. Next morning, 7 November 1307, they reconvened and continued their examination of William Cragh. They were now on the trail of causes: had William Cragh had "any vision or revelation from or by any saint or dead people or those who are in the other world?" He had. On the morning of his execution, while he was sleeping in the dungeon, the Virgin Mary had appeared to him, accompanied by a lordly figure. Mary was covered with precious stones and had a white stole around her head, but was not carrying her son in her arms "as shown in material images." William could not remember what clothes her companion was wearing.

There were thirteen prisoners in the dungeon and the Virgin Mary asked if there was anyone there called William ap Rhys. Yes, answered William, and Mary then told them all to climb up a ladder that had appeared there; all, that is, except Trahaearn. When William asked the Virgin Mary what he should do about Trahaearn, she replied simply, "You should leave him." The other prisoners, William explained, were all pardonned and freed that day. When questioned about the saint who accompanied her, she said that it was Saint Thomas who was liberating him.

At this point the commissioners became vigilant. William Cragh had presumed the saint was Thomas de Cantilupe. But there are other saints called Thomas, notably Thomas the apostle and Thomas Becket, the martyred archbishop of Canterbury. How did William Cragh know that the saint was Cantilupe rather than any other? William explained that before his imprisonment he had been on pilgrimage to Cantilupe's tomb in Hereford. Moreover, on the day that he was imprisoned he had, "following the custom of England," bent a penny "to the honour of Saint Thomas so that he should liberate him." This penny he had hidden in his belt and had managed to keep with him in prison and even on the gallows. Moreover, throughout his imprisonment and on the way to execution he had called aloud on the aid of Saint Thomas de Cantilupe.

William Cragh was making it clear to his questioners that he had chosen his saint. From all the thousands of saintly intercessors, and from the various saints called Thomas, he had elected Thomas de Cantilupe as his special champion. The introduction of the Virgin Mary, as a kind of sponsor of the saint, was not unusual. She was by far the most important saint in medieval Europe and her cult was flourishing at this time. Roughly one in five English parish churches was dedicated to her and in the thirteenth and fourteenth centuries most great churches had special "Lady Chapels" erected in her honour—one of the commissioners, Ralph Baldock, was responsible for building the Lady Chapel attached to Saint Paul's cathedral and was eventually to be buried in it. Her image, usually with the Christ child, as William Cragh observed, could be found in every church. She was especially renowned for saving desperate cases.

William Cragh's testimony was the first to introduce a vision of the Virgin and Thomas de Cantilupe during William's imprisonment. Neither Lady Mary de Briouze nor her stepson nor the chaplain had heard of any such thing, although they did report that the Welshman had invoked the saint on his way to the gallows. All three had also said that, according to the hanged man's own words, a bishop in white garments had appeared to him while he was on the gallows and had helped him. The commissioners obviously referred back to the record of this early testimony (given in London almost four months before) and noted this. With William Cragh before them, it was now possible to cross-check this piece of hearsay. The result was surprising: "Asked if it had seemed to him, while he was hanging on the gallows, that some bishop or anyone else sustained or supported him on the gallows, he answered no."

The maze of testimony was becoming yet more puzzling. Lady Mary de Briouze had explicitly reported "that the hanged man had said that a certain bishop, as it seemed to him, supported him by the feet." Her stepson had been equally explicit, though varying the details: "He said he had himself heard William Cragh say, when asked what he had seen and felt when he was hanged and afterwards and how he had been cured, that it seemed to him that a certain white bishop, dressed in white vestments, had placed his tongue back in his mouth and thus he had recovered the breath of life." The testimony of the chaplain William of Codineston on this point agreed with that of Lady Mary, although he also added the detail mentioned by William de Briouze junior, that the bishop was said to be white and dressed in white vestments. More significantly yet, he described where William Cragh had made these statements about the visionary bishop helping him on the gallows—before the lord and lady de Briouze in the castle of Swansea.

What the de Briouze party reported in 1307 as the explicit statement of William Cragh fifteen, sixteen, or eighteen years earlier was thus explicitly denied by William Cragh himself in 1307. We have moved beyond the vagaries of memory and slightly differing recollections to outright contradiction. If the de Briouze witnesses are treated as three independent witnesses, then their testimony should outweigh that of William Cragh, but it sounds very much as if they are describing the same statement made on the same occasion, even if William de Briouze junior remembered it slightly differently from the other two. The scene shows a recently hanged Welsh robber or rebel brought before his lords and captors and examined about how exactly he had survived execution. He would, perhaps, be willing to agree to suggestions about how he had been saved. He might improvise a few details himself. And, whatever he said and was said to him, we know it had to be transmitted through interpreters. When the notaries recording the canonization process in 1307 jotted down what the de Briouze party reported William Cragh had said, they were making a simultaneous translation into Latin of the evidence the witnesses gave in spoken Norman French, recording their memory of a translation made to them of a Welshman's words fifteen to eighteen years earlier. Perhaps we should be less surprised at the contradiction in this testimony, than in the agreements.

It is perfectly clear that the witnesses were all very dependent on rumor, gossip, and report. They gave their own eyewitness accounts but these are often influenced by what they have learned from others. This was true of William Cragh himself; he might appear to be the star witness but, because he had been unconscious for the crucial period, he was as much a reporter of others' accounts as Lady Mary in her chamber or the fastidious priest, William of Codineston. When he had revived, William said, "he had heard it said publicly and generally" that Lady Mary had pleaded for his body, to bury it in the churchyard, and that his relatives had carried him off but could not get into the church and so had come to the house of Thomas Mathews (the first mention of the name of the burgess whose house had received the corpse), where the Lady Mary had had his body measured to Saint Thomas. After his miraculous revival William Cragh could take up the story, making the revealing comment, "Because he was resuscitated and had been given to the lady, he was not hanged again." In his eyes at least another execution had been a possibility and it was only the miraculous status of his survival and the patronage of the lady that prevented this occurrence.

William Cragh concluded his evidence by describing his convalescence and the journey of thanksgiving to Hereford; by telling how the miracle had become widely known, leading to an increase in pilgrimage, to the shrine and general moral reformation; and by denying that magic or trickery had in any way been involved. Once the interpreters fell silent, the commissioners undertook a physical examination: "They inspected William's neck very carefully and found no damage there, but at the tip of his tongue he had some redness, which, he said, happened on account of the hanging, through the pressure of his teeth."

After William Cragh had given his testimony, the commissioners turned to the other witnesses in the case. All five came from Swansea or its environs and had firsthand knowledge of

William Cragh and the hanging. One of them, John of Baggeham, was actually the captain of the execution squad, and had
accompanied the condemned men to the gallows with his troop
of armed horsemen. The others were Thomas Marshall, a poor
priest of Swansea; and three other local men, Henry Skinner,
Adam of Loughor, and John ap Hywel. Henry Skinner had been
at the foot of the gallows, while the priest, Adam, and John ap
Hywel had seen the hanging from a distance. All except Henry
Skinner had gone to see William Cragh's corpse in the house of
Thomas Mathews.

Their testimony adds several interesting details. Three of
them mention that Trahaearn ap Hywel, hanged alongside William Cragh, was "noble." Two explain that William de Briouze
forced William's relatives to hang him themselves—a particular
refinement of brutality. Thomas Marshall said that he had seen
a chamber attendant of Lady Mary de Briouze, named Matilda
de la Chapel, in Thomas Mathews's house when William
Cragh's body was there. She had a silver spoon and a silver bowl,
although he did not see her spoon out anything to William
Cragh. John ap Hywel, despite his Welsh name, had little sympathy for the hanged man, reporting that the crowd around William
Cragh's body in Thomas Mathews's house "rejoiced greatly, for
William had frequently been the leader of many evildoers."

With the exception of John of Baggeham, the witnesses had
much more to say about the hanging and the corpse than about
the miracle. Thomas Marshall had heard that William Cragh
had been measured to Saint Thomas, but that was all. He had
first come to know of William Cragh's vision only eight days
before giving testimony, when William Cragh himself had told
him about it. Similarly, Henry Skinner, who had been present at
the hanging but had not viewed the corpse, had heard tell that
the lady of the castle had measured William Cragh to the saint
but knew nothing more until almost twenty years later when they
had set out from Swansea to Hereford, to give their testimony to
the commissioners. On the journey William Cragh had told him
about his vision. At least some of the Swansea witnesses must
therefore have traveled together, comparing notes (as we shall see

again later). Adam of Loughor and John ap Hywel had both heard report of the measuring but knew nothing of the vision.

The longest and most detailed report came from John of Baggeham. He was the steward of William de Briouze's household in Gower and had the duty of ensuring that the execution went smoothly. At the time of the canonization inquiry he gave his age as "fifty and more," so he was a man in his mid-thirties when he conducted William Cragh and Trahaearn ap Hywel to the gallows. He had anticipated that their friends and family might make a rescue attempt, so he prepared a posse of ten men, mounted and armed. One was Henry of Scurlag, member of a colonial family of Anglo-Norman settlers that held the fief of Scurlage Castle in western Gower. The particular cruelty of having William Cragh hanged by his own relatives has already been mentioned and John of Baggeham was well enough informed to know their names and their relationship to William: Gruffudd Foel, his uncle; Dafydd Asser, his cousin; and Ithel, described simply as his kinsman.

After the hanging, which John of Baggeham describes in detail, he went to report the death of the two men to his lord in Swansea Castle. Then "Lady Mary asked for the body of William [Cragh], he did not know why." After William de Briouze senior had given his permission, John of Baggeham was instructed by the Lady Mary to cut down William Cragh and take his corpse into the town. This he did, the body carried on the very ladder (not, it should be noted, on a wheel) up which he had climbed to the gallows. John then went to serve his lord at dinner. Next, before he himself could eat or drink anything, Lady Mary commanded him to take a thread she had obtained from the purse of her daughter Margaret and go to measure William Cragh to Saint Thomas de Cantilupe.

He found the body lying on the floor of Thomas Mathews's house, the eyes out of their sockets "as he saw likewise in the case of other hanged men," the tongue dark and swollen, with no sign of breathing. He touched the body and deemed that the man was truly dead. Then he stretched out William Cragh's arms and measured his breadth and length with the thread from the Lady

Margaret's purse. The house was crowded with men and women and many of them joined him when he prayed to God and Saint Thomas to restore the dead man's life. Not very long afterwards William Cragh moved a foot. Asked about it fifteen (or sixteen or eighteen) years later, John of Baggeham could not remember which one.

He went to report all this to the Lady Mary, who was over-joyed. John the steward was of a different opinion; he knew William Cragh from of old and was as pleased with his death as those who, according to the testimony of John ap Hywel, were so delighted at seeing the Welshman's corpse. "He had said to her," he reported, "that she was rejoicing about an evil thing, for it was evil that an evil man should be brought back to life." Despite his personal views, he had to follow his lady's commands, so they all went back to Thomas Mathews's house—Lady Mary, Lady Margaret her daughter, and the knights and squires and other members of her household and that of her husband. A great baronial retinue was now crowding into the burgess's house (Lady Mary herself says nothing of this visit). According to John of Baggeham, Lady Mary and Lady Margaret both insisted on measuring William Cragh to Saint Thomas again. Soon afterward he was able to close his eyes. They then left him for the night but returned in the morning with a nourishing almond purée. By the third day William Cragh was able to speak.

John of Baggeham's testimony is especially valuable, as he was obviously both hostile to William Cragh and unsympathetic to the attempt to invoke saintly aid for him. He said he had heard nothing about any vision; nor did he mention William's invoking the saint on the way to the gallows (although he might not have understood Welsh in any case). John simply describes the religious practices going on, in which he was forced by his station to participate. He does not understand his lady's motives nor approve her actions but has to play his part in the revival of the hanged man just the same.

4

An Autumn Day

The central incident in the story of William Cragh is his execution, and the tenacious questioning by the commissioners allows more light to be shed on the details of this grisly subject than can be obtained from any court records of the time. After his capture William Cragh was, according to his own account, accused of multiple homicides and, although he denied the charges, William de Briouze senior commanded him to be hanged. Hanging was the standard punishment for homicide in England at this time and the Anglo-Norman Marcher lords of Wales, who ruled lands conquered from the native Welsh, had the uncontested right to inflict it.

In the March of Wales, however, it was possible for compensation to be paid for homicide and for the condemned man to be redeemed by a payment of money or goods. As William de Briouze junior put it, "It is the custom in the land of Wales that those who are about to be hanged can escape with a payment if the temporal lords who have sentenced them to be hanged agree." In fact, according to this Marcher lord, such a proposal had actually been made, for the kinsmen of William Cragh and Trahaearn ap Hywel had offered his father a hundred cows for their lives. William de Briouze senior had been unwilling to accept the ransom. This piece of evidence contradicts one of the statements of John of Baggeham, the captain of the execution squad, who explained that Trahaearn was hanged after William because they were waiting to see if his relatives would offer a redemption payment to William de Briouze. They hanged him only when no offer was forthcoming. It is of course likely that not everyone involved in the affair would know everything that was going on, and William de Briouze junior and John of Baggeham might well both be stating the truth as it was known to them at the time. In native Welsh law sixty-three cows was the compensation payment for killing a noble, and an offer of a hundred cows was thus very substantial and quite credible as the combined price for the lives of a noble (Trahaearn) and a non-noble (William Cragh).

Setting aside the timing of events on the day of the hanging (a subject discussed later in this chapter), a synthesis of the reports of the nine witnesses presents the following picture. William Cragh and Trahaearn ap Hywel were led out of their prison in Swansea Castle—William in shirt and breeches, his noble fellow prisoner in a tunic—their hands tied behind their backs. Since William Cragh reported that he bore the rope with which he was to be hanged to the gallows, this must have been around his neck. There was then an uneasy wait while the posse under the command of John of Baggeham armed and mounted. On the way to the gallows William confessed his sins to a Welsh priest, Madog, the rural dean of the area. It could not have taken long to reach the gallows, which were located on a hill not far from the castle and within sight of onlookers on the walls and in the town square of Swansea. One of the witnesses, Adam of Loughor, was on the wall; another, Thomas Marshall, at the west gate; and a third, John ap Hywel, in the square with a hundred others. Presumably this easy visibility explains the placement of the gallows.

William Cragh and Trahaearn ap Hywel were treated differently, in both the choice of executioners and method of execution. As already mentioned, it was a particular refinement of William de Briouze's hatred that William Cragh was to be hanged by his own relatives. Trahaearn, by contrast, was in the hands of men described as "the town executioners." Although William Cragh was hanged on a rope attached to the horizontal beam of the gallows (it must have been a structure composed of two tall uprights and a transverse member) and went swinging when the ladder on which he stood was kicked away, an attempt was made to haul Trahaearn up by throwing a rope over the beam and pulling him off the ground. This, according to several of the witnesses, was the reason the transverse beam broke, for Trahaearn was "large and heavy."

All of the witnesses, save one, agreed that William was hanged first and two of the eye witnesses mentioned, as had Lady Mary, that he voided his bowels and bladder. The collapse of the central beam of the gallows followed, on the hanging of Trahaearn. Most witnesses, including the two who were present at the gallows, reported that both William and Trahaearn were hanged again, one on one arm of the gallows, the other on the other. The chaplain, William of Codineston, reported that eventually the rope supporting William Cragh broke, but John of Baggeham, in charge of the execution, gave evidence that he had cut William Cragh down at the command of Lady Mary de Briouze.

The papal commissioners paid considerable attention to the actual means of execution—the rope and the noose. At the very beginning of the case, when Lady Mary gave her account of the hanging, she was asked whether William Cragh had been hanged "with an iron hook or with a noose of rope." The question, which suggests some degree of misapprehension of the nature of execution by hanging in England and Wales, may have been posed by one of the French members of the commission. The reason the commissioners were interested in the details of the rope and the noose was that they had to establish the fatal efficacy of the execution—otherwise William Cragh's survival would not have been miraculous. William de Briouze junior was eager to convince them on this point, revealing in the process some intimacy with the details of hanging. "The method of hanging men in this country," he explained, "is such that the hanged men die immediately after the hanging, because a noose with a slipknot is placed around their necks and the knot of the noose is at the back of their necks so that they are suffocated at once." An additional reason they could be sure that William Cragh had really been killed, he added, is that it was customary, if any subterfuge or trickery were discovered in an execution, that the executioner himself would be hanged in turn.

Other witnesses also had something to say on the subject of the noose, although, surprisingly, the condemned man himself could supply little more. He noted that the rope was thick and denied that there had been any tampering with the knot "to prevent him dying at once on the gallows," although he also said he did not know what kind of knot had been made in the rope. Others mentioned that the rope had a slipknot but could not be precise about exactly where the knot was placed on William Cragh's neck—this was important, for it was a belief at the time that a "man may live many hours on the gallows if the halter be adjusted above the apple of the throat." Several mentioned the ladder up which he climbed to the gallows before it was removed and he was left dangling. Two reported that his body had been carried off after the hanging on that same ladder.

John of Baggeham has more to say about motives than the other observers. After the collapse of the transverse beam, which he attributes not to a botched attempt to haul up the bulky Trahaearn but to the weakness of the structure, he reports that both men seemed to be already dead. They were hanged again for two reasons: first, "as an insult to their kin," second, because "according to the custom of the country" hanged men should not be removed from the gallows without the lord's leave. Eventually, as mentioned, he cut down the corpse of William Cragh at Lady Mary's command, the body having at that time "as much life as there is in a stone." While John of Baggeham's version of local custom was that hanged men could not be removed from the gallows without the lord's permission, Lady Mary was equally certain that "it is the custom in those parts that when hanged men are dead they are taken down from the gallows." The contradiction may be merely apparent, John emphasizing the authority by which the corpses could be cut down, his mistress rather the fact that they were not left to rot on the gallows (as was the custom in some other times and places).

The fate of Trahaearn is not clear. Lady Mary says he was buried at the gallows, William de Briouze junior merely that his father commanded him to be buried, and the chaplain William of Codineston that he was carried off to Saint John's Chapel along with William Cragh. Nor is there unanimity about what happened to William Cragh's body. His relatives were, of course, present at the scene, having been forced to act as his executioners, and two of the witnesses assert that it was they who removed the body. Apart from the curious uncertainties about how he was carried off—on wheel, ladder or otherwise—there are slight ambiguities about the exact sequence of events that brought the hanged man to Thomas Mathews's house in the town, some positing a visit first to the chapel of Saint John the Baptist, others an unsuccessful attempt to enter the church, others not mentioning anything other than the fact that he was carried into town. In any case, there is no doubt that the corpse was eventually brought to the house of the burgess Thomas Mathews.

A Victorian textbook on medicine and the law describes the physical results of hanging:

> lividity and swelling of the face, especially of the ears and lips, which appear distorted: the eyelids swollen, and of a blueish colour; the eyes red, projecting forwards, and sometimes partially forced out of their cavities . . . a bloody froth or frothy mucus sometimes escaping from the lips and nostrils . . . the fingers are generally much contracted or firmly clenched . . . the urine and faeces are sometimes involuntarily expelled at the moment of death.

Almost all these symptoms are reported by one or more of the witnesses in the case of William Cragh. The long account by William de Briouze (in chapter 1) describes the lividity, protruding eyes, and blood around the lips and nostrils. The priest Thomas Marshall had been on his way to vespers when he noticed the crowd in Thomas Mathews's house. Going in, he had seen William Cragh's body lying stretched out on his back. "His eyes had come out of their sockets," he reported, "and his teeth were clenched so tight that some of William's relatives who were there were unable to open his mouth." Thomas Marshall himself had not touched the body to see if it was warm or cold but he was convinced the man was dead. Adam of Loughor, who was the youngest of the witnesses and could only have been thirteen years old or thereabouts at the time of the hanging, deposed that "he saw William lying on the ground stretched out and dead, covered with a cloak except for his face, and William's eyes were hanging out of their sockets and part of his tongue was sticking out of his mouth, clenched fiercely between his teeth, lacerated and black, and he saw in him neither movement nor breath, but he did not dare to come too close to him out of fear."

John of Baggeham was tougher and more experienced. He described William Cragh lying prostrate with his eyes hanging out of his sockets "just as he saw in the case of some other hanged men." The tongue was dark, swollen, and crushed between William's teeth and there was no trace of breathing or any other vital sign, "although he and others touched the body and when they all touched and observed him, they said and deemed that he was dead." John then proceeded to stretch out the arms of the corpse in order to measure the dead man to Saint Thomas de Cantilupe. As captain of the posse and steward of William de Briouze in Gower, John was obviously familiar with corpses.

To summarize once more, the procedure involved in the hanging of William Cragh was as follows: the condemned man was led to the gallows in shirt and breeches, with the noose around his neck and his hands tied behind his back. He was allowed to confess. At the gallows, which consisted of two uprights and a cross beam, he mounted a ladder and the rope was fastened to the beam. There is no mention of a blindfold. The ladder was removed and the hanged man swung until dead. His body was eventually cut down and his relatives took it off for burial.

One of the greatest discrepancies in the witnesses' accounts is the length of time all this took. Almost all give indications of the time of day that William Cragh was led out to be hanged, of the time he was actually hanged, and sometimes of when he was cut down. The measure they frequently employ in referring to time of day is that of the canonical "hours," the church services that marked out the liturgical day. Hence Lady Mary says that, although she did not know personally when William Cragh had been hanged, she had heard that it was "between Prime and Terce." On a November day that would probably mean around 7:30 A.M. Her statement fits reasonably well with those of William de Briouze, her stepson, who timed the hanging to Prime; and William Cragh himself, who might have best reason to know, and reported that he was conducted to the gallows "around the hour of Terce." Thomas Marshall, the poor priest, also said the condemned men were led out when Prime was well advanced (*post altam primam*). An early morning gallows scene is of course conventional in both fact and fiction.

Another set of voices confuses the issue, however. Several of the witnesses claim that it was later in the day that William was led out or hanged. Adam of Loughor said it was "around midday" when the condemned man was led to the gallows, Henry Skinner that he was hanged "soon after midday," while John of Baggeham and John ap Hywel both placed the hanging around or soon after "the hour of none," which at this period might mean either midday or the canonical hour of Nones, a little later in the afternoon. William de Briouze also refers to "the hour of none," but gives it as the time when news was brought to him and his father in the castle hall that the gallows had broken. He further identifies the time as "when people had eaten." In the same way, John ap Hywel places the hanging at the time "after the hour of none, because he had then eaten."

It is hard to believe that the condemned pair were led out at 7:30 A.M and hanged on a nearby gallows at midday, even though this is exactly what one witness, Thomas Marshall, asserts. John of Baggeham, in charge of the execution, notes two occasions for delay during the proceedings: one, when the ten-man posse was being armed and mounted, and another, after William Cragh had been hanged, while they were waiting to see if Trahaearn's relatives would offer a redemption payment. It is still hard to turn all this into a five- or six-hour process. The bodies were taken down, according to Thomas Marshall, "around halfway between the hour of none and sunset," and according to William de Briouze at sunset, which would be around 4 P.M. in Gower in November. John de Baggeham, who, as we have seen, was not in favor of the attempt to save William Cragh's life, reports that, after he had cut down the corpse and sent it off to the town at Lady Mary's request, he had returned to the castle "to serve his lord, who was then at dinner in the castle." This clearly refers to the second meal of the day. John complained that after his lord had eaten he himself had not had a chance to eat or drink anything before his lady sent him off to measure William Cragh to Thomas de Cantilupe. It had been a long day.

Death by Hanging

T
he accounts of the execution offered by the witnesses in the canonization process harmonize well with other accounts and depictions of hangings from the medieval period. Pictorial representations show that the typical gallows does appear to have been constructed of two uprights and a crossbeam, as was the case in the hanging of William Cragh and Trahaearn. For instance, one of the most unforgettable illustrations of execution by hanging, that from the early-twelfth-century *Miracles of St Edmund*, now in the Pierpont Morgan Library in New York, shows eight thieves dangling from a crossbeam, which is stretched between two roughly hewn forked uprights. One of the two executioners actually sits astride this beam. The thirteenth-century monk, Matthew Paris, who illustrated his own historical writings, adds to his account of the hanging of the garrison of Bedford Castle in 1224 a sketch of the unlucky soldiers dangling from the gallows. Its structure is precisely the same as that in the Pierpont Morgan manuscript, except that it contains two crossbeams with three roughly hewn forked uprights supporting them. Most medieval images of this kind of scaffold, as in these two examples, show the crossbeam simply resting on the fork of the uprights, but a few depict carefully carpentered joints supported by diagonal struts. Obviously the gallows erected in William Durand's bishopric of Mende to symbolize the cooperation of king and bishop, with one leg on the bishop's lands and the other on the kings' (mentioned in chapter 2), must have been of the "two uprights and crossbeam" variety.

The two Welshmen who went out to be hanged outside the walls of Swansea were dressed, respectively, in shirt and breeches and in a tunic. The dress of the hanged men in medieval illustrations ranges from ordinary full costume to shirts to loincloths. These latter are found in many pictures, from the Pierpont Morgan illustration of the early twelfth century to an Italian painting from the school of Perugino at the very end of the Middle Ages. It may be that stripping the condemned man was sometimes the practice, and one English writer of the thirteenth century does indeed state that the hanged man's clothes were a perquisite of whoever performed the hanging, but it is also worth remembering that the most common representation of an execution scene in medieval art—even though it involved a method of execution long since abandoned—was the crucifixion of Jesus and the two thieves, who were conventionally depicted in loincloths. Perhaps the iconography of that scene sometimes shaped the way medieval artists depicted hanged men of their own epoch.

William Cragh went to the gallows with the noose around his neck, a practice that can be shown to have been followed in other penal settings of the Middle Ages. The records of the Grand Châtelet, the central Paris prison, in 1488 and 1489, mention two prisoners "taken to the gallows, rope around their necks." As we have seen, William Cragh and Trahaearn ap Hywel were bound when they were led out of Swansea Castle but were not blindfolded at or before the gallows. At the Châtelet binding the hands in front of the body was apparently more shaming than binding them behind. If the same conventions applied in colonial Wales as in France, the Welshmen were spared this additional humiliation. The thieves in the Pierpont Morgan manuscript are blindfolded (it looks as if caps have been pulled down over their eyes) and have their hands bound, some in front of and some behind their bodies and, although the small scale of Matthew Paris's drawing makes details less distinct, it seems that the Bedford garrison were also blindfolded and bound. Other illustrations of hangings confirm that binding the condemned man's hands was an almost universal practice, although blindfolding seems to have been less common.

At Swansea the site of the gallows was a hill outside the town. There was a long tradition of execution at such spots—Golgotha itself was "a green hill . . . without a city wall." Those condemned to death in London during the medieval and early-modern periods were usually taken outside the city walls to Tyburn, near the present Marble Arch, while in Paris the path to the gallows lay down the Rue Saint-Denis and out of the city. Likewise, in early modern Germany scaffolds were usually located outside the town walls. At Vienna only the honorable form of capital punishment, beheading, took place in the market square, while the more violent forms, involving breaking the prisoner's limbs with a wheel, were carried out beyond one of the city gates or at the so-called wheel-crossing in the Vienna hills. The choice of hilltop outside the town at Swansea separated the place of execution from the usual everyday environment, yet still made the hanging public and visible. It also entailed the procession to the gallows, a ritual with many dramatic possibilities—as we have seen, it was while making his way to the scaffold that William Cragh confessed to a local Welsh priest. Several medieval Welsh towns had such a "Gallows Hill" half a mile or a mile outside the town.

One of the curiosities of William Cragh's execution is that he was hanged by his own relatives, constrained by William de Briouze senior. Trahaearn, by contrast, was strung up by "the town executioners." Clearly there were official hangmen at Swansea but others could be forced to do the work, too. Writing in the early part of the thirteenth century, Thomas of Chobham, sub-dean of Salisbury, claimed, certainly with some exaggeration, that there were no official executioners in England but that "someone who is met on the way is forced to hang the condemned man." The execution at Swansea exemplifies a particularly cruel instance of such coerced novice executioners.

Before the elaboration of "the drop," a collapsible platform or trapdoor, in the eighteenth century, hangings was effected by the condemned man's being "turned off" a ladder or cart. In the case of William Cragh it is explicitly stated that he climbed up a ladder, which was then removed. This seems to have been standard practice and several medieval illustrations of hangings show the ladder propped up against the gallows. At Newenham Abbey in Devon four tenants held their land in return for the duties of, respectively, conducting the prisoner to the gallows, putting up the gallows, supplying the ladder, and doing the hanging. One ingenious variation on the ladder is depicted in an English manuscript of the eleventh century, which shows the two uprights of the gallows with projecting footholds up which it was possible to ascend.

In contrast to William Cragh, Trahaearn was not "turned off," but pulled up by a rope cast over the crossbeam—it was this, according to several witnesses, that caused the beam to break. As in the case of the ladder, images of this procedure can be found in medieval depictions of hangings. A manuscript painting of the late eleventh century from the monastery of Saint Amand in Flanders shows a hanged man, in loincloth and with hands bound behind his back, being pulled up by two executioners with ropes across the crossbeam, while an illustrated thirteenth-century *Sachsenspiegel*, a German law-book, depicts a Jew being hanged by being hauled up by a thick rope over the crossbeam.

Lady Mary de Briouze was asked if William Cragh had been hanged "with an iron hook or with a noose of rope." It is not certain what exactly can be inferred from this question. The corpses of dead criminals, including those who had been hanged, were not infrequently suspended in chains until they rotted, the chains obviously serving to keep the decomposing body in place for as long as possible, but the reference in the canonization process is clearly to a method of execution rather than a way of displaying a corpse. Presumably the iron hook is being pictured as a kind of collar rather than a meat-hook. There are instances of hanging in which something other than a rope was used. A man who was to be hanged at Worcester in 1184 "had an iron chain placed around his neck while the executioners prepared to haul him aloft." Whether the chain was expected to suffocate him or whether he was to be left to die of exposure, starvation, and strain is not clear. Similarly, when a bunch of robbers and killers, headed by a renegade man-at-arms, was executed in 1366, the leader "was hanged with an iron chain, the others with ropes."

The illustration of the hanging of the thieves from the Pierpont Morgan manuscript shows what could be interpreted as iron collars around the men's necks. They dangle from ropes, or possibly thin chains, which hang from rings placed over pegs on the crossbeam. One of the executioners, in what is actually a physically pointless act, is seen hauling on a rope or chain attached to one of these pegs. The text which the picture illustrates simply says, "they were fastened to the gallows." A yet more perplexing case is the eleventh-century account from southern France mentioning a man hanged by "*wooden* nooses" (my emphasis). It seems there were a variety of ways of going to one's death on the gallows. As we shall see in chapter 12, the son-in-law of William de Briouze junior was himself executed by being hanged with an iron chain.

Many centuries after William Cragh's hanging there is evidence from Carmarthen, not far from Gower, of the belief that a man who had survived hanging should not be hanged again. William Calcraft, public hangman from 1829 to 1874, had to carry out a hanging there in the first year of his office. At first attempt the rope broke and the condemned man, David Evans, fell down. Onlookers cried, "Shame! Let him go!" and Evans himself said, "I claim my liberty. You have hanged me once and you have no power or authority to hang me again. It is against the law to hang me a second time." "You are greatly mistaken," replied Calcraft, "My warrant and my order are to hang you by the neck until you are dead. So up you go, and hang you must until you are dead."

Such disputes about the repetition of hanging can be found in the legal theorizing of the Middle Ages, too. An Italian jurist writing around the time of Cantilupe's canonization process argued that repetition of hanging after the rope had broken was only permitted if the judge had specifically condemned the victim to be hanged "until dead" (very much Calcraft's point). Another, writing in the second half of the fourteenth century, thought that if the rope broke after a saint had been invoked, this was probably an indication of a divine miracle and the condemned man should be freed. English kings of the thirteenth and fourteenth centuries appear to have shared this view, at least on occasion. When a man survived hanging in 1234, the English chancery records explain that "his life has been saved through the divine mercy," while Edward III, issuing a charter of reprieve in similar circumstance in 1363, remarked, "God has given you life and we will give you a charter." In the account of William Cragh's execution and resurrection there is only a slight hint of such a belief; this is when Lady Mary de Briouze says, in words already cited, "This man has been hanged twice and has suffered a great penalty. Let us pray to God and Saint Thomas de Cantilupe that he give him life and, if he give him life, we will conduct him to Saint Thomas." Otherwise, there is no sense that survival of hanging gives the condemned man the right to his life. When the beam of the gallows breaks, William Cragh is strung up again from the remaining arm of the scaffold (and, according to some witnesses, so is Trahaearn).

Hanging was a standard form of execution in the medieval period, at least from the eleventh century onwards. Of those ninety-eight prisoners condemned to death at the Châtelet of Paris in the years 1389–92, sixty-eight were hanged. Of the others, fourteen were burned, twelve decapitated, three buried alive, and one boiled in a cauldron. In this case, hanging thus represented nearly 70 percent of all executions. In one sense William Cragh and Trahaearn were lucky. Although they faced death by hanging, they did not endure the particularly gruesome forms of execution that were being elaborated at this period, to punish those who defied the king of England. Already in the time of Henry III (1216–72) there are cases of capital punishment inflicted on traitors in especially grisly ways. The outlaw and pirate William de Marisco, who was suspected of plotting to assassinate the king, was dragged to the gallows behind a horse (Matthew Paris provides a vivid picture of this as well as an account of these proceedings), and was then hanged. When his corpse had stiffened, it was cut down and disembowelled, the entrails burned. The shattered body was cut into four parts, each of which was sent to one of the chief cities of the kingdom "so that this wretched sight should strike fear into all who saw it."

Henry III's son and successor, Edward I, was equally vindic-
tive in his treatment of those who rebelled against him. The executions of the last Welsh prince, Dafydd ap Gruffudd, in 1283,
and of the Scottish resistance leaders William Wallace and
Simon Fraser in 1305 and 1306, showed the same practice of
inflicting on the condemned man "not one but many deaths."
Dafydd was dragged by horses as a traitor and hanged as a killer;
his entrails were burned as a punishment for sacrilege; and,
"because he had plotted the death of the lord king in many
parts of England," his corpse was cut up and the pieces sent
throughout the land. His head was stuck on a pole atop the Tower
of London. William Wallace was given identical treatment, with
the addition that he was beheaded "as an outlaw." The quarters
of his corpse were sent to Newcastle upon Tyne, Berwick, Stir-
ling, and Perth, "for the terror and chastisement of all who pass
by and see them." If William Cragh had been, in the words of
William de Briouze, a "rebel against the lord king," he was luckier
to have fallen into the hands of de Briouze than those of the
ferocious Edward I.

Thus, in many ways there was nothing unusual about William
Cragh's execution. Perhaps more surprisingly, there are also
plenty of parallels to his miraculous revival from hanging. A few
years before the Cantilupe inquiry, in 1300, an Italian man called
Cecco, who had got mixed up with a thief in the town of Capua,
was hanged along with the thief. Two guards kept watch by the
gallows "from morning until evening." Returning from their duty
at dusk, they were startled to find that Cecco was following them,
with the noose around his neck, crying out, "Saint Zita, help
me!" When he was brought before the authorities, Cecco described how the figure of a lady had appeared to him, and supported him by the feet as long as the guards were present and
that, as soon as they had left, she had broken the rope and said
to him "Go! Go!" "For fear of God and Saint Zita," said the saved
man, he should be released and allowed to go to Zita's shrine in
Lucca. He declined to have his clothes, which had been taken
from him before the hanging, returned, and went just as he was
with the noose around his neck. The record of his ordeal, and

the sight of his legs, black and swollen with blood, became part of the case for Zita's sanctity (a serving girl who had died in 1272, ten years before Thomas de Cantilupe, she was to be recognized as the patron saint of domestic servants).

The parallels with the case of William Cragh are clear. As in at least some versions of the events at Swansea, the saint supported the hanged man on the gallows. A similar pilgrimage of thanksgiving to the saint's shrine, with the noose still around the saved man's neck, then followed the miracle. There are also significant differences, however. William Cragh was saved by the typical English medieval saint, a highborn male ecclesiastic; Cecco by a type of saint, a lowborn, female layperson, that was never truly common but was more common in Italy than elsewhere. Although Cecco, like William Cragh, was hanged alongside another condemned man, who did not benefit from the saint's intervention, the narratives describing these two events stress different points. The account of Cecco's miraculous survival makes much of the fact that, while the thief hanged alongside him was guilty, Cecco himself was innocent and had confessed to involvement in the crime only after torture. Saint Zita thus intervened to protect the innocent. William Cragh did indeed persistently avow his own innocence of the homicide and arson charged against him, but he seems to have been the only one to believe in it. None of the other witnesses, including Lady Mary, who pleaded for his life, regarded him as anything other than a brigand or rebel. It is not that Trahaearn, the man who was hanged and died, was guilty, and William, the man who was hanged and survived, innocent.

Analysis that has been undertaken of forty-two cases of miraculous salvation from hanging in the medieval period shows an intriguing pattern. Of the nineteen men saved from hanging in the period 550–1100, fourteen were described in the sources as guilty, four as protesting innocence and in one case there is no clear indication. By contrast, in the period 1100–1500, the pattern is reversed: there are five guilty, fourteen innocent, and four uncertain. Hence, in the early medieval period about three-quarters of those the saints saved from hanging were presented as guilty of the crime for which they were being executed, while in the later medieval period a minimum of 60 percent were presented as innocent. It is not easy to explain this development, although it may be, as has been argued by the author of the analysis, that over the course of the Middle Ages the Church became gradually more reconciled to the righteousness of secular justice and hence saw the exercise of saintly grace more properly where an innocent was condemned than when a criminal was snatched back from death. In the case of William Cragh, however, his guilt or innocence is an almost peripheral matter compared with the main focus of the inquiry: had he been truly dead?

Pictorial representations of miraculous salvation from hanging sometimes show saints supporting the hanged man by placing their hands beneath his feet, holding him around the legs or body, or, in one case, holding him up by the hair. Saint Nicholas of Tolentino is depicted in one late medieval Italian painting performing the delicate task of balancing two hanged men, one on each hand. Nicholas, a friar from central Italy who died on 10 September 1305, less than a year before Clement V initiated the canonization process of Thomas de Cantilupe, had something of a reputation for this type of miracle. One case, dating to the years 1305–26, involved two brothers wrongfully accused of murder in the southern Italian town of Aquila. Torture wrung a confession from them and one of the brothers was hanged. Four days later, when the executioners came back to the gallows to hang the second brother (the delay is not explained) they found not a rotting corpse but a living man. He was cut down, the miraculous power of Saint Nicholas recognized, and the two brothers went free.

Two centuries later Nicholas of Tolentino was still busy saving hanged men. In 1505 two thieves were executed on the gallows in Bologna. When they were taken down for burial, it was found that one of them was alive, even though the noose had cut deeply into his throat. This lucky survivor was visited in the hospital by the senators of the city, to whom he described how Saint Nicholas of Tolentino had supported him by placing his hands under the soles of his feet. In thanks, a votive offering of a picture of the hanged man, together with the noose with which he had been hanged, was placed in a local chapel, while the man himself became a member of the Order of Augustinian Hermits, to which Saint Nicholas had belonged.

In many of the cases of miraculous salvation from hanging, the saint intervenes in the way we have seen, supporting the hanged man, and thus allowing him to survive on the gallows until he is taken down. Sometimes, as in the case of Cecco and Saint Zita, the saint breaks the rope. A particularly instructive case of this type is found among the miracles of Saint Elizabeth of Thuringia (d. 1231) reported in January 1235 as part of her canonization proceedings. These include two cases of miraculous salvation from hanging. In one of them a man who is wrongly accused of theft is hanged from a high oak tree. While a real thief hanged alongside him dies, the innocent man invokes Saint Elizabeth and the rope from which he is suspended breaks. When an attempt is made to hang him again the judge rules, "He whom God has freed is not to be hanged again." Here again is that hint of the feeling expressed by the unhappy David Evans at Carmarthen, that when the rope broke, the hanged man had a right to go free. It was definitely not, as we have seen, a feeling that was allowed to have any sway in the case of William Cragh.

William Cragh's case was not simply a miraculous salvation from hanging but a genuine resurrection. It was not a matter of the hanged man surviving on the gallows or the rope breaking, but of a death followed by return to life. The right saint had obviously been invoked, for the record suggests that resurrection of the dead was especially frequent among the miracles performed by Thomas de Cantilupe. The canons of Hereford were able to present to the commissioners a list of forty resurrections achieved by their saint—a remarkable number, since it was not a commonplace form of saintly intervention. Indeed, a careful study of 4,756 miracle accounts from eleventh- and twelfth-century France found only sixty cases of resurrection; that is, 1.26 percent. Thomas de Cantilupe's forty is thus a number equivalent to fully two-thirds of the miraculous resurrections over these two centuries in France. It is worth noting, however, that resurrections grew more common over the course of the Middle Ages. While they form only 1.26 percent of miracles recorded in eleventh- and twelfth-century France, they constitute 2.2 percent of miracles examined in thirteenth-century canonization processes and 10.2 percent in fourteenth-century ones. Resurrections were still a rarity but they were subject to a slight inflationary drift. The canons of Hereford clearly represent a local case of hyperinflation.

Time and Space

At the very beginning of this study it was observed that the first three witnesses in the case, the de Briouze party, did not agree on the timing of the execution and the miracle. Lady Mary de Briouze thought these events occurred in winter about fifteen years earlier, though she was uncertain of the exact day and month; William de Briouze said that William Cragh had been captured between Michaelmas and All Saints' Day next, eighteen years ago; and the chaplain, William of Codineston, dated them to sixteen years earlier. The second group of witnesses, the six men heard at Hereford, also produced varying estimates of when the hanging had occurred. In addition, many of the nine witnesses gave differing accounts of how much time passed between the hanging and the visit of thanksgiving to Hereford cathedral. Table 1 illustrates the varying testimonies of the nine different witnesses.

It is worth noticing that all six of the witnesses heard at Hereford date the hanging to the Monday after Martinmas, and all except William Cragh to sixteen years earlier (although Thomas Marshall was not certain about this). Their agreement could be interpreted as strong evidence in favor of their accuracy, but it should also be remembered that Thomas Marshall's knowledge of William Cragh's vision had been imparted to him by William Cragh himself only eight days before he gave testimony, and that Henry Skinner had been told about it by William Cragh "while they were coming to give evidence on this matter." At least some of the witnesses had thus traveled from Swansea together and

Table 1. Evidence of the Witnesses on the Date of the Hanging and the Convalescent Period

Witness	Date of Hanging	Time Convalescing
Mary de Briouze	"about fifteen years ago . . . in winter" winter 1291 or winter 1292	"several days"
William de Briouze junior	"eighteen years ago between Michaelmas and All Saints' next" October 1289	"five weeks or so"
William of Codineston	"sixteen years ago" 1291	"eight or ten days"
William Cragh	"fifteen years ago on the Monday after Martinmas next" 17 November 1292	"a week or more"
Thomas Marshall	"on a Monday around Martinmas fifteen or sixteen years ago" November 1291 or November 1292	
John of Baggeham	"sixteen years ago . . . on the Monday after Martinmas" 12 November 1291	"after a month he would say"
Henry Skinner	"the Monday after Martinmas next sixteen years ago" 12 November 1291	
Adam of Loughor	"the Monday after Martinmas next sixteen years ago" 12 November 1291	
John ap Hywel	"the Monday after Martinmas next sixteen years ago" 12 November 1291	"after a month"

talked over the distant events. Moreover, it has been pointed out that witnesses in canonization processes sometimes exhibit a kind of "mimicking," which "incites the witnesses to take up the formulae of the first among them." Indeed, one of the greatest of the medieval canon lawyers warned explicitly against letting witnesses in canonization proceedings "be informed by another and follow him." These considerations might explain their unanimity as to date, although it leaves the loose end of William Cragh's "fifteen years"—unless this is a mistake in the translation from his Welsh.

Two points are worth making about the way the witnesses dated these events. First, no one, not even the chaplain and the priest, gave a year in the *anno domini* form; that is, "1289" or "1291." Such dating was common in documents of the time and must have been familiar to barons and clergy but they, just as much as the Swansea laborer, located events by stating how long ago they had taken place. To give the subjective measure of distance from the speaker's present was more natural for them than to mark an objective point in a sequence of the years. Second, it is clear that there was much greater agreement about the time of year William Cragh was hanged than about the year. Although the six witnesses heard at Hereford all dated the hanging to November, William de Briouze said William Cragh and Trahaearn ap Hywel were captured in October, and Lady Mary thought these events took place "in winter" (she could not remember the month), they do offer the consensus of winter.

These two features, the marking of time by measuring distance from the present and the high memorability of time of year, also emerge in the so-called Proofs of Age, inquests that took place in England at exactly the same period as the canonization process of Thomas de Cantilupe and were designed to ascertain whether a minor heir had reached the age to inherit his property. A few years before the canonization process, in October 1301, such an inquest was held by the sheriff of Sussex into the age of Roger, son of Adam de Bavent, who claimed to be of full age and therefore able to enter into his inheritance. Roger was born at Wiston in the Rape of Bramber, into an important landholding family, which had long connections with the de Briouzes. In 1301 twelve jurors from the towns and villages around Wiston, all of them men aged thirty or more, gave evidence as to Roger's age. The fullest testimony was from the first juror, Ralph of Catwick, "aged fifty and more," from Steyning, only a mile and a half from Wiston. He said

> that the said Roger was twenty-one on Friday before the Annunciation last, and was born at Wiston and baptized in the church there by a priest named John; and William Bernhouse, Roger de la Hyde, and Eva of Cumbe were his godparents; and he knows of the heir's age because he is his next neighbor, and has a son John who was born three years and more before and was 25 at the feast of the Nativity of Saint John the Baptist last.

The value of Ralph's testimony rests upon a personal association—the birth of his own son. He knows when this was and can then link it to Roger's birth. Since Ralph's son was twenty-five at his last birthday and was born three years before Roger, Roger must be over twenty-one. Years are identified by their distance from the present, days by their ecclesiastical feasts. It is possible for modern historians, with the aid of calendrical charts, to state that Roger was born on 24 March 1280 and Ralph's son John, on 24 June 1276; but that is not how Roger or John would think of their birth dates.

The eleven other jurors in this Proof of Age all provided equally personal recollections, often, like Ralph, mentioning the birth of their own children, or sometimes other family events: John le Graunt from Henfield knew Roger was of full age "because Robert his father, whose heir he is, died on the eve of Saints Philip and James, twenty years ago, and the heir was born a year and more before"; William Testard, "aged sixty and more," from Steyning, "says that three years and more after the heir's birth he married one Maud, eighteen years ago at the feast of Saint James last." One of the jurors had attended Roger's baptism, another the "churching," when the mother first visited church after the birth. The wife of another juror had been the baby's wet nurse. All these connections built up an air of credibility in the testimony. As a result of the hearing, Roger was indeed allowed to enter his inheritance.

Setting the evidence from the canonization process beside that from the Proofs of Age, we can see how the people of early-fourteenth-century England structured their memory of time by distance in years from the present, by memorable personal incidents, and by the landmarks of the great Christian festivals. The jurors in the case of the Sussex landholder Roger were, of course, specifically summoned to give evidence on the one issue of the heir's age, while for those in the canonization inquest the date of the incidents were of only subordinate interest, and this may well explain the willingness of the commissioners to tolerate slight discrepancies or vagueness in their testimonies about dates.

It would be understandable if our analysis of the testimonies in the case of William Cragh simply concluded that different people remember dates differently, some more precisely, some less; we can go further, however. Apart from the record of the resurrection of William Cragh made at the canonization inquiry of 1307, there is another, and this one was made by the canons of Hereford at the time of the incident. We therefore have a contemporary as well as a retrospective account. What is even more remarkable is that it forms part of a record of Cantilupe's miracles kept in chronological order and with many miracles actually dated.

It reads as follows:

[1290] On 2 December the nobleman Lord William de Briouze and his wife, along with their household and in the presence of many people, came to the tomb of the man of God. They established through many trustworthy witnesses that a certain young man, William Cragh of Gower in the land and lordship of this lord, had, on 26 November, been judicially condemned to be hanged, and that, when he heard this, the young man devoutly sought refuge in the help of God's servant. He prayed that he would seek for him from God on high a longer space of time to do penance and reform his ways and he had a penny bent to God's servant. Behold! When the officers deputed to hang him had hanged him regardless, immediately the rope from which he was hanging broke and he fell to the ground, half-dead. When they had hanged him again, in a short time the transverse beam of the gallows snapped in the middle and he fell to the ground, dead at that time, as they said. Nevertheless, the officers hoisted a rope to one post of the gallows and cruelly hanged him for a third time and waited around him, with a great crowd of people, until they were absolutely certain of his death. Then everyone went home, leaving him hanging on the gallows. Afterwards, the relatives of the hanged man came to the lord and sought leave to take down his corpse and bury it. This was granted and he was taken down and carried to the grave. When they had begun to bury him, suddenly to the amazement of all he revived, pulled in his hands and feet and began to speak. When he was asked by many of them how he had revived, he answered clearly and distinctly, "I confess that my life has been restored to me by God on high through the merits of the holy bishop Thomas de Cantilupe." When they heard this, all who were present at this sight gave most devout thanks to God and his servant.

This account of Cantilupe's miracles, maintained by the canons of Hereford in chronological order, thus gives us an absolute chronology. William Cragh was sentenced on 26 November 1290 and the de Briouze party arrived in Hereford to give thanks on 2 December 1290. If the journey from Swansea to Hereford had taken three days, as Lady Mary and John of Baggeham said and which is plausible for a distance of sixty miles, then William Cragh had convalesced for only three or four days.

There are other contrasts between this luckily extant, contemporary report and those given by the witnesses in 1307, besides the discrepancy in date. According to the Hereford account, William Cragh was actually hanged three times, and was being buried when he showed signs of revival. None of the witnesses confirms these statements in 1307. The bending of the penny is, however, mentioned, and, overall, it might be concluded that the main difference between the contemporary account and the evidence at the canonization hearings lies not in contradictions but in omissions. The Hereford story is streamlined.

One reason for this is that the canons of Hereford wanted a simple story reflecting the power of their saint. They did not go into what time of day the execution took place, how the knot was fastened around William Cragh's neck, or on what contrivance he was carried from the gallows. They needed to establish three things: prior invocation of Thomas de Cantilupe, the fact of death, and the fact of revival. The names and dates were recorded for further verisimilitude but there was no cross-examining of witnesses, no checking of discrepancies. The commissioners of 1307 were investigating a case, the canons of Hereford in 1290 rejoicing at a further demonstration of the power of God's servant resting in their cathedral.

The contemporary account gives the date of the sentencing as 26 November 1290, a Sunday. The general consensus of the witnesses seventeen years later was that the hanging had taken place on a Monday. The discrepancy is only apparent, however, for the exact words of the contemporary account are that "William Cragh . . . had, on 26 November, been judicially condemned to be hanged." He then, of course, faced a night in jail before being led out to execution, so condemnation on Sunday, 26 November was followed by execution on Monday, 27 November. What cannot be reconciled is the witnesses' insistence that the hanging occurred on the Monday after Martinmas, for Martinmas falls on 11 November, which was a Saturday in 1290, so 27 November was in fact the third Monday after Martinmas. Perhaps the significance of the feast, which was one of the more important in the year, had drawn the witnesses' memory by a kind of gravitational pull, inducing them to place the event in immediate rather than merely close proximity to the great feast-day.

If Monday, 27 November was the date of the hanging and the de Briouze party arrived in Hereford on 2 December, the following Saturday, after a three-day journey, then William Cragh had been convalescent from only Monday to Thursday. Two of the witnesses, John of Baggeham and John ap Hywel, reported that this period was "a month or more," and William de Briouze junior, who had been a member of the party going to the shrine at

Hereford, said that it was "five weeks or so" between the hanging and the journey. It may be that this inflation in the estimated length of the convalescent period resulted from an unconscious wish on the part of the witnesses to emphasize how dreadful was William Cragh's state and hence how marvelous was the intervention of Saint Thomas de Cantilupe, but the remembering of a three-day period as a five-week period, even after a gap of seventeen years, is extraordinary. There is another indication of numerical imprecision on the part of William de Briouze. He reported seeing William Cragh many times over the course of "ten years and more" after the hanging and that the Welshman had died a natural death "around two years ago." Since he also reports that the hanging occurred eighteen years earlier, his "ten years or more" plus "around two years" should add up to eighteen.

A much less extreme inflation is found in the memories of William of Codineston and William Cragh himself, who give closely comparable estimates ("eight or ten days," "a week or more") for the convalescence period. William Cragh was, of course, in the party that traveled to Hereford, although the chaplain William was not. It is Lady Mary who reports the shortest and most accurate length for convalescence. She had taken charge of his care during this period and would thus have a day-by-day knowledge of his needs and condition, although, as is clear in the case of her stepson, personal involvement and accurate recall are not inevitably associated.

Now that we have established the exact date of the hanging and of the journey of thanksgiving , an unexpected fact swims into view: issuing sentence on William Cragh was one of the last things William de Briouze senior did. The journey to Hereford was the first stage of the last journey of his life. On 2 December he was organizing the gift of a wax gallows at the shrine in Hereford. Exactly five weeks later, on 6 January (Epiphany), 1291, he died in his manor house at Findon in Sussex. William of Codineston was rector of Findon at the time of the canonization process of 1307 and perhaps was already so in 1291. As family chaplain he may have given William de Briouze the last rites. On 12 January 1291 the royal government instructed Robert de

Tibetot, Justiciar of South Wales, to take the lordship of Gower into the king's hands because of the death of William de Briouze, and on 2 March commanded him to give possession of the lord-ship to William de Briouze junior. A few weeks later William and his stepmother made an agreement about her dower, that is, the lands of her late husband that she would hold until her death, of which Findon was part.

One reassuring consequence of knowing that William de Bri-ouze senior died in January 1291 is that it confirms that the canons of Hereford were accurate in the date of William Cragh's hang-ing as recorded in their chronologically arranged miracle collec-tion. They placed it in November 1290. In contrast, seven of the nine witnesses from 1307 situate the event in November 1291 or November 1292. Although this might seem a weighty body of evidence, they cannot be right. Even Lady Mary de Briouze is not exact about the time of her husband's death, or else she would have given a more precise date to the hanging than "about fifteen years ago." Only William de Briouze junior gives a time frame ("eighteen years ago") that places the incident unequivocally in a period when we know his father was actually alive. Establishing an exact date for the miracle was not, as mentioned, the prime purpose of the papal commissioners investigating the case, but it is still striking that William de Briouze senior's death, an im-portant family event and one that concerned a central figure in the story, was never mentioned by any of the witnesses.

We can now say that the witnesses of 1307 were thus being interrogated about an event that had occurred almost seventeen years earlier. Obviously relevant to the question of their powers of recall over time is their age at the time of the event. The papal commissioners asked the age of each of the nine witnesses in the case except the Lady Mary, so their ages at the time of the inci-dent can be established (it is not clear why Lady Mary was not asked her age—other female witnesses were). The results appear in table 2.

The evidence about ages shows that the majority of the wit-nesses were recalling events which had taken place while they were definitely adults. Only two were teenaged at the time of

Table 2. Age of the Witnesses in 1307 and 1290

Witness	Age in 1307	Age in 1290
William de Briouze junior	46	29
William of Codineston	45	28
William Cragh	45	28
Thomas Marshall	32	15
John of Baggeham	50	33
Henry Skinner	34	17
Adam of Loughor	30	13
John ap Hywel	40	23

the hanging. However, all of the witnesses, except for Thomas Marshall and Henry Skinner, are explicit that the ages they report are approximations: "forty-five, or around that," "fifty years and more," or, in the (translated) words of William Cragh, "he does not know for certain but he estimates that he is forty-five years old." This explains the statistically unlikely preponderance of numbers ending in a zero or five among the ages given: five of eight of them (62.5 percent), whereas in the population as a whole the proportion with ages of a multiple of five would be two out of ten (20 percent). They are obviously rounded figures. The fact that the two witnesses who do not state that they are making an approximation give ages of thirty-two and thirty-four, which are not multiples of five, fits this assumption well, although it should be noted that even they may be engaged in the attested medieval practice of rounding to an even number. In a survey of the population of two parishes in Rheims in 1422, 83 percent of the population gave their age as an even number!

In addition to testifying about their own ages, two of the early witnesses whose evidence was heard at London, when William Cragh was still presumed dead, give an estimate of his age. Lady Mary said that William Cragh was about thirty years old (presumably at the time of the hanging), while her stepson maintained that he seemed to him to be around forty years old. If William Cragh's own testimony is to be believed, then the lady was far more accurate than her stepson. Given his record of imperfect recall this is not surprising, though it may be relevant that William de Briouze had seen William Cragh on many occasions after the hanging, indeed until the time he would have been, by his own estimation, forty years old. Perhaps the mental picture of the older William Cragh eclipsed that of the hanged man.

Of course, being inaccurate about someone else's age is different from being inaccurate about one's own. The evidence of the witnesses in this case suggests that even a great baron of the thirteenth or fourteenth century would not know his exact age. This implies that, even if his birthday were celebrated, there would be no clear idea of *which* birthday it was. The Proofs of Age, discussed above, support the idea that exact age was something that needed to be investigated and proven rather than simply assumed. The imprecision about how long ago the hanged man had been hanged was matched by the witnesses' imprecision about how old they were.

The witnesses also included in their testimony mention of far shorter units of time, little periods of the fateful day in question. The terminology they use reveals some interesting aspects of their concepts of time. Measures of time frequently employ terms that belong to the world of physical extension: "length of time" and "space of time." The word commonly employed by the witnesses in the canonization process to refer to short periods was rendered in the notaries' Latin as *spacium* (or *spatium*). In origin, *spacium* meant "a racecourse" (it is related to the word "stadium") and had progressed to the more general "walk, promenade," then to "a distance, length" and had finally been borrowed to refer to duration—"a space of time." It is not likely that the witnesses knew this etymology but, curiously enough, the way they measure "a space of time" is often by describing how far one could walk in that period.

John ap Hywel, for instance, reported that William Cragh was on the gallows before Trahaearn was hanged "for the space that he estimates a man could have gone a quarter mile or so." The second hanging lasted "for such space that he estimates he could have gone a quarter mile." Henry Skinner said that William Cragh was on the gallows before Trahaearn hanged "for the space that he estimates a man could have gone a quarter mile at an ordinary pace." He had stayed watching after the second hanging "for such space that he could have run a mile." John of Baggeham uses this kind of indication of time frequently: Trahaearn was hanged after William Cragh had been hanging "for such space as he estimates a man could have gone a quarter mile"; after invocation of Saint Thomas, William Cragh moved "quickly thereafter, so that a man could have gone as he estimates a furlong or an eighth part of a mile"; during his recovery William Cragh shut his eyes "for such a space as a man could have gone a mile, as he estimates."

There is no mention by any witness of hours or minutes as measures of duration. Although they used the canonical hours of the day to mark out moments in the course of the day, as discussed in chapter 4, when they were asked "how long," their answer took the form "as long as it takes to. . . ." Just as the Proofs of Age show how points in the past were identified by subjective associations rather than by objective *anno domini* dating, so the witnesses' testimony illustrates how small units of time were defined by the personal measure of experienced duration—how long it takes to walk half a mile—rather than an objective numerical scale of minutes and hours.

A particularly telling instance of this kind of thinking can also be found in the miracles of Saint Elizabeth of Thuringia, which have already been mentioned because of the cases of salvation from hanging that they include (chapter 5). In one of them the uncle of the hanged man gave the following evidence: "He thinks that he had hanged on the gallows for the space of one German mile." He must clearly mean "for the length of time it takes to go one German mile," although even in the Middle Ages the passage was misunderstood and transposed to describe the distance of the gallows from the town. His instinct, however, of conveying duration of time by reference to space covered, is exactly that of the witnesses in the Cantilupe proceedings.

Just as time could be measured by space (for example, as long as it takes to walk a mile), so too space could be measured by time. Both Lady Mary and the steward John of Baggeham describe Hereford as being "three day's journey [*tres dietae*]" from Swansea. With distances of this kind, reference to traveling

time is more natural than a figure in miles. It is easier to estimate and more useful to the traveler; just as modern American
custom is to describe places as "three hours away," that is, a three
hours' drive, so medieval travelers would think in terms of a
"day's journey."

Hereford was a long way from Swansea and the distance could
be measured in "day's journeys." The witnesses also give indications of much shorter distances. Since they were giving testimony
regarding a hanging, their location at the time was important;
what they could see would be affected by where they were standing. Apart from William Cragh, two witnesses (John of Baggeham and Henry Skinner) were at the gallows, Lady Mary and
William de Briouze junior were in Swansea Castle, Thomas
Marshall was at the town's west gate, Adam of Loughor on the
wall, and John ap Hywel with one hundred others in the square.
It is not clear where William of Codineston was during the
hanging, but he had encountered William Cragh on his way to
the gallows. Most witnesses give some estimates of the distances
involved.

They have two methods of giving linear measures. One is to
use standard units of measurement, such as the mile. We have
already seen them using miles, quarter-miles, and furlongs when
giving estimates of time, and it was obviously also natural for
them when talking of short distances. The distance from the
town or castle to the gallows is given as "about quarter of a mile"
by William Cragh and John of Baggeham, and the distance from
the town square to the gallows, which would be a little greater,
is estimated at "half a mile" by John ap Hywel. Once again William de Briouze junior differs in his estimate, saying the gallows
were "about half an English league" from the town and the castle.
A league was generally three miles and, if that is the case here,
William de Briouze estimated the distance to the gallows as a
mile and a half, six times that given by William Cragh and John
of Baggeham, both of whom had travelled from the castle to
the place of execution on the morning of the hanging (although
William Cragh must have had reason to find the journey too
quick). However, a league could also, though less commonly,

mean two miles or even a mile and a half, and, if this is the unit William de Briouze had in mind, the discrepancy between his assessment and the others' becomes slighter. It may be significant that the only other witness to use the league rather than the mile as a unit of measurement is Lady Mary, when giving the distance from the gallows to the chapel of Saint John as "half an English league." Possibly it was a more aristocratic custom to measure in leagues rather than miles.

Apart from giving standard units of linear measurement such as the mile and the league, the witnesses also frequently used a stock comparative measure—the length of a crossbow shot. Thomas Marshall reported that the gallows "can be seen from the castle and the town and they are about two crossbow shots away from the castle," while the west gate of the town, where he stood, was "about one crossbow shot from the gallows." Henry Skinner said the gallows were "two straight shots of a good crossbow" distant from the castle, Adam of Loughor that the gallows were "two crossbow shots as he estimates" from where he stood on the town wall.

Three points can be made about this way of giving a distance. First, it is vivid, pictorial, and basically non-numerical. One could imagine a distance by imagining oneself standing and firing a crossbow. It did, of course, create a unit, the crossbow shot, that could then be multiplied ("two crossbow shots," etc.), but it gave distance by referring to a human activity over space, not to a mere scale. Second, it seems that it was the length of a *crossbow* shot that came to the mind of these men of Swansea, not that of a longbow. In 1290 the longbow, which was fostered in south Wales before it became a standard weapon of English armies in the later Middle Ages, was just about to begin its murderously successful career as a chief weapon against the Scots and the French (the first notable victory in which it was decisive was Falkirk in 1298). These townsmen turned for a gauge of distance not to this battle-field weapon of such future importance, but to the customary armament of town guards and garrisons. Because of their slow loading time, crossbows were employed more often from protected spots, such as town or castle battlements, than from the open field. Third, the information given in the testimony allows some equations to be drawn between standard units of measurement and the length of a crossbow shot. The distance from the castle and the town to the gallows is described by several witnesses as a quarter of a mile and by several as two crossbow shots. The length of a crossbow shot is being pictured as 220 yards; not an ambitious range but a plausible one.

The world of the witnesses, while not lacking some fixed scales of measurement, thus shows a preference, both in time and space, for subjective yardsticks rather than objective ones. Numerical precision was less common than reference to personal experience as a template by which temporal and spatial location could be given.

Colonial Wales

More than two centuries of conquest, colonization, and resistance lay behind the relations of power revealed in the case of William Cragh. A frontier between the English and the Welsh had first been created as a result of the Anglo-Saxon settlement in Britain. By the early seventh century the Celts of Wales were cut off from their linguistic kinsmen in Cornwall and Cumbria. The great symbolic line of Offa's Dyke was built in the eighth century. This was not a watertight frontier, but it formed an approximate and traditional dividing line between the English and the Welsh. In the wake of the Norman conquest of England in 1066 this line lost its significance as the Norman barons who had conquered and carved up England sought to do the same to Wales. They fought the native Welsh princes, built castles along the coasts and in the river valleys, and brought in settlers from outside. In the east and the south of the country, especially, new colonial settlements arose and new colonial lordships were established.

The lordship of Gower was formed in the early days of Norman expansion in Wales. Normans were raiding the area by 1095, they killed its Welsh ruler in 1106, and they maintained castles at Swansea and elsewhere in Gower by 1116. The first lords were the Beaumont earls of Warwick, members of one of the greatest Anglo-Norman baronial families. William, earl of Warwick, who died in 1184, apparently pledged Gower to the king in return for settling his debt to the Jews. It was never reclaimed and was in royal hands until 1203, when King John granted it to William de

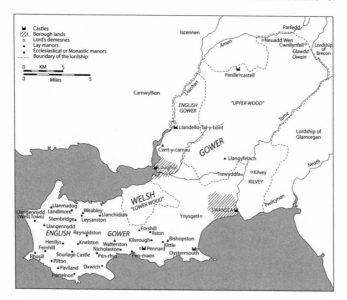

Fig. 2 The lordship of Gower

Briouze (d. 1211), ancestor of the two Williams involved in the hanging of William Cragh.

Over the course of the twelfth and thirteenth centuries the landscape and culture of Gower were transformed by settlers from England. Not only did new lords and their followers inhabit the twenty or so castles that, at one time or another, dotted the coasts and lowlands, but also numbers of English peasant farmers tilled the richer, arable parts of the lordship and townsmen lived in the new boroughs of Swansea and Loughor. They brought with them the English language. The imprint of this new settlement is marked on the map by the English place-names that predominate in the southern part of the lordship of Gower. Gower was divided administratively into "Welsh Gower" and "English Gower": the parts where native Welsh settlement was relatively undisturbed and Welsh tenurial arrangements persisted, on the one hand, and the colonized and manorialized areas, on the other. The geographical division was not simple, for

Welsh Gower was in two parts (the "Upper Wood" and the "Lower Wood") and Welsh men and women continued to live in parts of English Gower.

Both William Cragh and Trahaearn ap Hywel came from the parish of Llanrhidian in the Gower peninsula. The name is, of course, Welsh, and probably means "the church of Saint Rhidian." It was one of the larger parishes in the lordship and replicated on a smaller scale the ethnic divisions of Gower as a whole. The southern and western parts of the parish were characterized by such English place names as Walterston ("Walter's farm or estate") and Weobley. At the latter site there is a small stone castle, and it may have been named after the place of the same name in Herefordshire, whence, no doubt, many of the English settlers came. In contrast, the hilly northern and eastern sections of the parish constituted part of "Welsh Gower" (the "Lower Wood") and its place-names, such as Bryngwas and Wernhalog, suggest an entirely native population. The moor that rises to the northeast of the church, separating the two parts of the parish, was called (from at least the seventeenth century, but probably much earlier) the "Welsh Moor." The parish church of Llanrhidian, along with the chapel at Walterston, was granted to the Hospitallers (Knights of Saint John) in the twelfth century by William de Turberville, who was also responsible for endowing them with the churches of two neighboring parishes. He was obviously an important Anglo-Norman landholder in Gower and almost certainly the man listed among the knightly vassals of the earl of Warwick, the lord of Gower, in 1166. His estates consisted of both more heavily settled and anglicized parts, and tracts where the Welsh had been left in occupation of the land.

The divisions between native and settler discerned in the parish of Llanrhidian were found throughout Wales. In the period 1066–1282 the country was divided between territories ruled by native Welsh dynasts, such as the princes of Gwynedd and the descendants of the princes of Deheubarth (southwest Wales), whose seat was at Dinefwr (fewer than twenty miles north of Swansea), and the Marcher lordships such as Gower. Boundaries shifted from year to year, with endemic small-scale and occasional large-scale warfare. Yet the pattern of alliances and enmities did not invariably follow ethnic lines, for there were disputes within and between the native dynasties (as there were between the Marchers) while intermarriage between Marcher families and Welsh princely dynasties did take place, even if it did not often prevent future hostilities between the parties. The political and military situation was ever-changing.

The history of Gower was as violent as that of any contested part of Wales. It may have been occupied by the Anglo-Normans by 1116 but it was continually vulnerable to counterattack from native Welsh forces. Indeed, the first mention of the lordship of Gower, in 1116, is in a record of an attack by Gruffudd ap Rhys of the house of Deheubarth in which he burned the outer parts of Swansea Castle. Twenty years later, as part of the general uprising of the Welsh after the death of Henry I in 1135, there was a native offensive against the "coastal region called Gower, which is very pleasant and fruitful," the attackers defeating a force of more than five hundred settlers that confronted them. It may even have been the case that the area was completely lost to the Anglo-Normans at that time, for a later tradition records a member of the house of the earls of Warwick reconquering Gower during the reign of King Stephen (1135–54). By 1151 Gower was again under Anglo-Norman control, although again subject to raids from the sons of Gruffudd ap Rhys.

During the reign of Henry II (1154–89) an agreement between the king and Rhys ap Gruffudd, son of Gruffudd ap Rhys, secured a long period of relative peace in southern Wales. The position of the Welsh prince (known as the "Lord Rhys") was recognized and the settler lordships on the coast enjoyed freedom from attack. This all came to an end at the death of Henry II in 1189. The Lord Rhys started ravaging Gower that same year and three years later he made a determined effort to capture Swansea, besieging it for ten weeks, until the threat of a large army advancing from England and the dissension among his own sons induced him to withdraw. The Deheubarth dynasty continued to harass Gower after the Lord Rhys's death in 1197. In 1212 Swansea was burned by one of his sons, Rhys Gryg, and in 1215 a grandson,

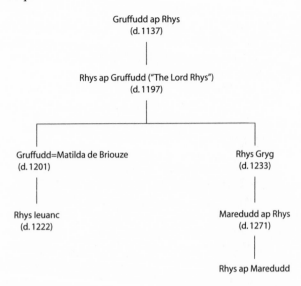

Fig. 3 Family tree showing members of the Deheubarth dynasty
mentioned in the text.

Rhys Ieuanc, "gained possession of all the castles of Gower," including the most important of the de Briouze castles, Swansea
and Oystermouth. The complexity of the politics of the time is
shown by the fact that, while Rhys Ieuanc's father was the Lord
Rhys's eldest legitimate son, his mother was not a Welsh no-
blewoman but a member of the de Briouze family, Matilda,
daughter of William de Briouze, the man who received the lordship of Gower from King John.

The transmission of Gower in the early thirteenth century
was complicated by quarrels between members of the de Briouze
family as well as the threat from the native Welsh. William de
Briouze was granted Gower by King John in 1203 but five years
later fell out of favor and lost it, along with all his other lands.
The family was able to recover it, however, and the lordship of
Gower eventually came into the possession of two of his sons in
succession, Giles and Reginald, the latter being the son-in-law
and ally of Llywelyn ap Iorweth of Gwynedd, the most powerful

of the Welsh princes. In 1217 Reginald made his peace with the English royal government, and in retaliation Llywelyn ousted him from Gower and gave it to Rhys Gryg of Deheubarth, the same man who had burned Swansea five years earlier.

As son of the Lord Rhys, Rhys Gryg took the princely traditions of Deheubarth seriously. He had his seat at the ancestral castle of Dinefwr and brought into his own hands several of the constituent parts of the old kingdom of Deheubarth. In Gower he made a determined effort to erase all trace of the previous hundred years of English settlement: "He destroyed the castle of Swansea and all the castles of Gower and their fortifications and he expelled all the English population that was in that land without hope of their ever coming back again, taking as much as he pleased of their chattels and placing Welshmen to dwell in their lands." That this was policy rather than racism is suggested by the fact that in 1219 Rhys Gryg married the daughter of Earl Gilbert of Gloucester, English lord of the neighboring Marcher territory of Glamorgan. In that same year Llywelyn ap Iorweth of Gwynedd gave a daughter in marriage to John de Briouze, the nephew and rival of Reginald de Briouze, his other son-in-law. Llywelyn had by now made his peace with the English government and was even ready to dispossess Rhys Gryg at its request. After he did so, in 1220, he gave Gower to John de Briouze.

The house of de Briouze was thus given Gower by the king of England, deprived of it by that same king and restored to it again, deprived of it by the prince of Gwynedd and then restored to it by him, all within seventeen years. Once John de Briouze acquired Gower in 1220, however, he hung onto it until he died, in 1232. His death was due to an accident—he fell from a horse at his other main lordship, Bramber in Sussex—and his son and heir, William, was a boy at the time and did not come into his majority until 1241. Then he took up his full powers as lord of Gower, powers that were eventually, many years later, to include passing a sentence of death on William Cragh.

During the long tenure of power by William de Briouze senior, the lordship of Gower experienced the growing strength of Llywelyn ap Gruffudd, prince of Gwynedd (1246–82). He aspired to the position held by his grandfather, Llywelyn ap Iorweth, and launched campaigns against Welsh rivals and Marcher lords alike. In 1257 his targets included Gower: "In Lent he came with a great army to Kidwelly and Carnwyllion and Gower and he completely burned the part belonging to the English in those lands, along with Swansea, and he subjected to himself all the Welsh of those lands." One of his allies was Maredudd ap Rhys, son of that Rhys Gryg who had sought to implement ethnic cleansing in Gower in 1217–20. In the summer of 1257 two hundred of the English settlers in Gower were killed. Llywelyn's alliance with Maredudd ap Rhys did not endure and a fierce rupture ensued between the two men, but Llywelyn was successful in asserting his domination of Wales and this was recognized by the king of England in the Treaty of Montgomery in 1267. The king acknowledged Llywelyn as "Prince of Wales" and conceded to him the homage and fealty of all the Welsh lords (except Maredudd ap Rhys).

Before the later thirteenth century the king of England had intervened militarily in the governing of Wales at times, but more commonly left situations to be resolved locally. Only under Edward I was a determined attempt made to destroy native Welsh power, now concentrated almost entirely in the hands of the prince of Gwynedd. In 1276 and 1277 Edward's armies defeated Llywelyn and forced him to accept a considerable reduction in his territories. William de Briouze participated in the campaign. For a while it looked as if there might now be a stable understanding between the Welsh prince and the king but Edward was not an easy man to have as a lord; in 1282 Llywelyn was provoked into rebellion and the immense resources of the kingdom of England were harnessed to annihilate independent Wales. The last prince of Gwynedd was killed and his territories became part of the newly created Principality of Wales, a royal dominion that included the counties of Anglesey, Caernarfon, and Merioneth in the north, and Cardigan and Carmarthen in the south. The rest of Wales remained in the hands of the Marcher lords. William de Briouze was unable to participate in person in the campaigns of 1282, being on pilgrimage to Santiago in Spain, but a force of 360 men from Gower, led by a de Briouze vassal, did take part.

The history of the lordship of Gower in the twelfth and thirteenth centuries shows the tenacity of both the English colonial settlement and the efforts of the native Welsh, notably the dynasty of Deheubarth, to overthrow the colony and reclaim Gower. Periods of peace were rare and periods of security rarer. Swansea was attacked repeatedly and burned more than once. In every generation members of the Deheubarth princely family attempted to reverse the Anglo-Norman annexation of Gower.

All this is necessary for a full understanding of the story of William Cragh. According to John of Baggeham's account, William Cragh was incarcerated by the lord of Gower "because he was said to have been present with many others at the attack and burning of the lord's castle of Oystermouth." Oystermouth was a de Briouze castle on the coast south of Swansea and the only recorded occasion when it was attacked in the relevant period was in 1287, during the rebellion of Rhys ap Maredudd. A chronicler from south Wales reports that in June 1287 Rhys ap Maredudd seized the castle of Dinefwr, burned and plundered the town of Swansea, and then, on 27 June, "seized and burned the castle of Oystermouth." These are the precise political circumstances in which William Cragh committed the homicide and arson of which he was accused.

Rhys ap Maredudd, who rose in rebellion in 1287, was the son of Maredudd ap Rhys of Deheubarth, the man who had been ally and then enemy of Llywelyn the Last, and whose homage was explicitly reserved for the king of England in the Treaty of Montgomery. Rhys himself had fought on the side of Edward I against Llywelyn in 1277 and again in the final crisis of the house of Gwynedd in 1282. He could easily be portrayed as a Welsh turncoat, a traitor to the "national" cause, like those Scottish lords who bowed to Edward I's authority in the 1290s while William Wallace defied him.

On the other hand, Rhys ap Maredudd had claims of his own as a direct descendant in the male line of the princes of Deheubarth: his ancestors included Gruffudd ap Rhys, who had assaulted the newly built castle of Swansea in 1116; the Lord Rhys, who ruled much of the old kingdom from the ancient seat of Dinefwr and had almost captured Swansea by siege in 1193; and Rhys Gryg, the scourge of English Gower, "helm of Dinefwr . . . lion of combat." Maredudd, Rhys's father, facing the rising power of Llywelyn of Gwynedd, had veered between alliance and defiance. Tried and imprisoned by Llywelyn in 1259, he was freed only when he had handed over his son as a hostage and surrendered the castle of Dinefwr, the seat of the Deheubarth princes. At his death in 1271, Maredudd still possessed the castle of Dryslwyn, but the rights to his homage had just been transferred to Llywelyn by the English Crown and he had not regained Dinefwr, which was held by another branch of the family. Rhys ap Maredudd, his son, had reason enough to chose Edward I rather than Llywelyn of Gwynedd.

One of the early events in the war of 1277 was a royal expedition in southern Wales. Rhys ap Maredudd negotiated an agreement with its leader: he would give all the military assistance he could to the royal forces and in return the king of England would promise to consider his claim to Dinefwr and other appurtenant lands, if they came into the king's hands. Rhys remained loyal to King Edward in the next and final confrontation with Llywelyn. As a native chronicler remarked, in the war from 1282 to 1283 "Rhys ap Maredudd held with the lord king, wherefore he kept his lands and received wider ones from the lord king, while everyone else was disinherited." He did not, however, obtain Dinefwr. What was even worse for his princely aspirations, he was actually forced to make a formal renunciation of it. On 16 October 1283, in the royal manor house of Acton Burnel, Rhys ap Maredudd renounced any claim to the castle of Dinefwr "for ever." His support for the English king had not brought him all he wished and his sense of grievance festered.

Apart from his disappointed claim to Dinefwr, Rhys was irked by other aspects of the new regime in southern Wales. The king's Justiciar of South Wales, Robert de Tibetot, whom we have already briefly encountered (in chapter 6), was a man determined to enforce his and the king's rights of jurisdiction as he saw them. This involved applying English rules of law rather than native Welsh procedures—"wrongly compelling Rhys and his Welshmen to plead according to English law," in the words of one of Rhys's complaints to the king. A host of minor disputes over land and money added further friction. In September 1286 Rhys took a list of grievances to the king, who was then in his French duchy of Gascony. Edward was not unsympathetic but the machinery of royal government had its own momentum. Proceedings were brought against Rhys in the county court of Carmarthen and, when he failed to appear, Tibetot prepared for the next step in the procedure: declaration that Rhys was an outlaw. In the spring of 1287 the king ordered three of his judges to attend the county court of Carmarthen and examine the proceedings against Rhys. Even if these were in order, however, the sentence of outlawry was to be postponed. Edward was clearly not a simple partisan in this case; yet it was too late. On 5 June the three royal judges concluded that the proceedings against Rhys were in order. On 8 June Rhys ap Maredudd went into revolt and captured the castles of Dinefwr, Carreg Cennen, and Llandovery.

Once Rhys had openly become, in Edward's words, "a manifest rebel and enemy of the king," things were simpler. The powerful and elaborate forces of the English state could be directed to a clear and single goal—the repression of the rebellion and the extermination of its leader. Thousands of men were mobilized and the Italian merchants in London were tapped for vast loans. Meanwhile, Rhys made the incursion into Gower that was eventually to bring William Cragh to the gallows:

> He came down into Gower in the month of June with a great army and joined to him the Welshmen of that area who lived in the Upper Wood. In that same month by their counsel . . . he burned the town of Swansea . . . and a few days later descended on the noble manor of Oystermouth, which the brave knight Sir William de Briouze had built for himself, and—I do not know whether by force or by fraud—

he captured the castle there. Of the men who were taken prisoner, some he commanded to be killed in his presence, others he led off captive. Who can tell of such unheard of cruelty without weeping?

This is the description of the raid from someone who knew.

Although he was from the Lower Wood section of Welsh Gower, William Cragh evidently joined the men from the Upper Wood in adhering to Rhys and participating in the attack on Oystermouth. The tone of outrage in the extract from the chronicle just quoted fits in well with the hatred that many of the witnesses to the execution of William Cragh report or express. It is not surprising that William de Briouze, his retainers, and the inhabitants of Swansea would delight in seeing a participant in the raid of 1287 dangling on the end of a rope. The killing, burning, and looting of June 1287 would not be too distant a memory in November 1290.

The royal campaigns directed against Rhys ap Maredudd in the period of June 1287 to January 1288, in which Robert de Tibetot played a prominent part, virtually crushed the rebellion. Rhys was left without a fortified base and with few supporters. He was not captured, however, and for some years managed to survive, hiding and raiding, despite the price of £100 that Edward I had placed on his head. He even seems to have returned to Gower at some point, for in February 1289 the king wrote to William de Briouze and his bailiff of Swansea reporting that he had heard that "Rhys ap Maredudd, the king's felon and rebel, is received and maintained in William's land of Gower." William was commanded to have a proclamation made throughout his land prohibiting anyone from giving aid or support to Rhys and his men. It may be that William Cragh was one of those "receiving and maintaining" Rhys at this time.

After living as a rebel and a brigand in the woods and hills of southern Wales for almost five years, Rhys ap Maredudd was finally captured in the spring of 1292 by native Welshmen, who were well rewarded with grants of land. Rhys himself was taken to York; Edward I was there before continuing to Scotland to begin his long and fateful involvement with the succession crisis of that kingdom. On 2 June 1292 a group of justices tried Rhys for sedition, homicide, arson, robbery, larceny, and destroying the king's castles. He was found guilty, drawn through the streets, and hanged, his body left dangling for three days.

By this time William Cragh had already been hanged and revived. He may have been simply "a notorious brigand" in the eyes of Lady Mary de Briouze and her chaplain, but William de Briouze junior recognized him more precisely as "one of the rebels" in "the war between the Welsh and the lord king." William Cragh, a Welshman from Welsh Gower, had joined a descendant of the ancient dynasty of Deheubarth in a late and ill-fated rising against the English king and the Anglo-Norman colony. When he was led out from Swansea Castle to be hanged, on 27 November 1290, he was on a stage already marked by almost two hundred years of conflict over possession of the land. The building of the Norman castle of Swansea had provoked the attack by Gruffudd ap Rhys in 1116, and in 1290 the supporters of his great-great-grandson were being imprisoned and condemned there.

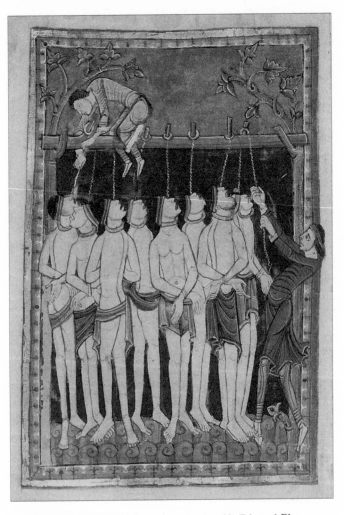

Fig. 4 Hanging of thieves, from the *Miracles of St Edmund*. Photo courtesy the Pierpont Morgan Library, New York. MS M. 736, f. 19v.

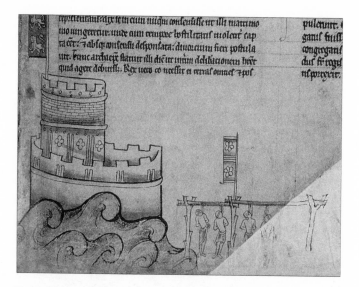

Fig. 5 Hanging of the garrison of Bedford Castle, 1224. Photo courtesy Master and Fellows of Corpus Christi College, Cambridge.

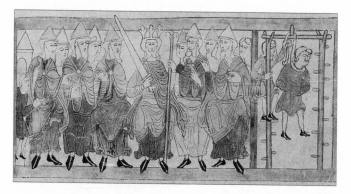

Fig. 6 Hanging scene from an eleventh-century English manuscript, Cotton Claudius B. IV, f. 59. Photo permission of the British Library.

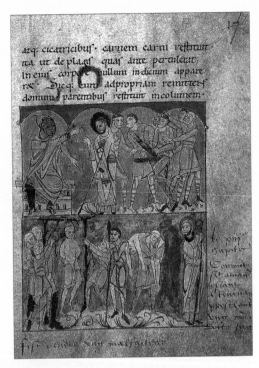

Fig. 7 Hanging scene from a manuscript from the monastery of Saint Amand. Photo courtesy Bibliothèque Municipale de Valenciennes.

Fig. 8 Hanging of a Jew from a thirteenth-century *Sachsenspiegel*. Photo courtesy University Library Heidelberg, Cod. Pal. germ. 164.

Fig. 9 Oystermouth Castle, the seat of the de Briouze family attacked in 1287. Photo courtesy Royal Commission on the Ancient and Historical Monuments of Wales

Fig. 10 Oystermouth Castle: aerial view from the southeast. Photo courtesy Royal Commission on the Ancient and Historical Monuments of Wales.

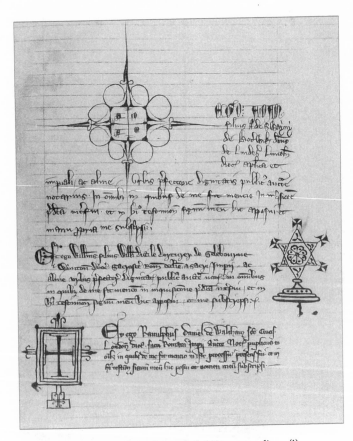

Fig. 11 Notarial signs from the canonization proceedings (i).
© Biblioteca Apostolica Vaticana vat. lat. 4015 264r.

decorem ecclesie vestre universalis ad cuius regimen conseruet uos ds p tempora p[ro]=
pera [et] longeua. Dat London sexto kl. Octobr. Anno dni. M. cc. Nonagesimo
quarto.

dño.

Sanctissimo patri ac dño reuerendissimo dei gratia sacrosc[t]e romane ac uniuer=
salis ecclesie summo pontifici Antonius eiusde dei miseratione ecclesie Dunelm
minister humilis cu debito honore [et] reuerentia pedu oscula beatorum. Quia feli=
cis recordationis pastor quondam pussimus dñs Thomas de Cantilupo
Herefordeñ nup Eps nobili prosapia ortus. a prime sue iuuentutis pri=
mordijs de uirtute in uirtutem ingrediens sic subsequenter in assumpti
talento regiminis pastoralis operatus est fideliter [et] p fecit sedm popularem opi=
nionem a famam diuulgatam quam p miracula de ipso publice predicata
credo et Coram qui iam in gaudio dñi sui braui beatitudinis eterne feliciter
apprehendit. Hec ute sanctitatis auribz constanter duxi insinuanda suppli=
cans deuotissime etiam ad maiorem laudem ure fidei ortodoxe. Vt super ten[i]=
tate de pmissis statuere dignemini circa eum qd cedate ad laudem [et] glor[ia]m
summi saluatoris. [et] decorem totius ecclesie universalis. Conseruet uos
deus omnipotens

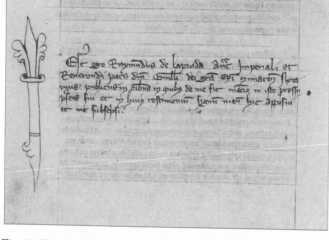

Fig. 12 Notarial signs from the canonization proceedings (i).
© Biblioteca Apostolica Vaticana. vat. lat. 4015 263v.

8

The Lord

William de Briouze junior, who gave his testimony to the papal commissioners in London in July 1307, was the direct descendant in the male line of one of the more important of the barons of William the Conqueror. He was well aware of this, for he was almost certainly responsible for commissioning an abbreviated copy of Domesday Book, that great survey of the estates of the king and the barons made at the Conqueror's command in 1086, and in the margins of this copy the note "Br'" identifies the manors of William de Briouze, the follower of William I. The description of the raid of Rhys ap Maredudd on Gower in 1287, quoted in the previous chapter, is written on the spare leaves at the back of the volume.

The family took its name from Briouze in southern Normandy, between Domfront and Argentan, and presumably this is where it had its earliest landed property. There is no explicit mention of William de Briouze fighting at the battle of Hastings in 1066 but he must have served his lord well, for William the Conqueror gave him lands that placed him among the twenty wealthiest barons of England. Apart from scattered holdings in Berkshire, Dorset, Hampshire, Surrey, and Wiltshire, he had the whole of the great Rape of Bramber, one of the six portions, running north to south, into which Sussex was divided. The northern part of the lordship of Bramber was Wealden woodland, slowly being penetrated by pig farmers, charcoal burners, and the like, but the southern part was crowded with rich and populous manors such as Washington and Findon. In 1086

Washington had a population of 150 peasant families, was a center of salt production and was valued at £50, five times the average worth of a Sussex manor. It was within the boundaries of this manor that William de Briouze chose to build the castle of Bramber. Nearby Findon, the village where his descendant and namesake died in 1291 and of which William of Codineston was rector in 1307, had over fifty peasant families and was worth more than £28. It had belonged to Harold Godwineson, the last Anglo-Saxon king, before his death at the battle of Hastings, forty miles along the coast.

The de Briouze family acquired great wealth through the Norman Conquest of England and it continued to expand its estates whenever it could. By the end of the eleventh century William's son, Philip, held lands in the March of Wales, though it is unclear how he acquired them. Over the generations the family added to its estates by some careful marriages to heiresses, acquiring half the barony of Barnstaple in the 1130s and the Marcher lordships of Brecon and Abergavenny in the 1160s. The de Briouze star reached both its greatest heights and its lowest depths under King John (1199–1216), who first raised up the current head of the family, yet another William de Briouze, to be one of the richest and most powerful men in the kingdom, giving him, among many other grants, the lordship of Gower; but then brought him crashing down, dispossessing him and driving him into exile, imprisoning and starving to death his wife and eldest son.

The very complex history of the years after the downfall of William de Briouze in 1208 has been briefly sketched above (in chapter 7), as part of the discussion of the transmission of the lordship of Gower in those years. Basically, the de Briouze family recovered most of its estates, with one share, including Brecon and other lands, going to one branch of the family; the other share, including Bramber and Gower, to another. The male Brecon line died out in 1230, leaving the lords of Bramber and Gower as the sole male representatives of this old baronial lineage. The head of this branch was John de Briouze, father of that William de Briouze who had William Cragh hanged.

William de Briouze senior was only eleven or twelve when his father died of a fall from his horse in the summer of 1232. For almost a decade thereafter William was a ward of the Crown, shuffled between courtiers and the king's relatives according to the prevailing political circumstances, until he came of age in 1241. Then, for the next fifty years, he ruled his lordships of Gower and Bramber, as well as other scattered manors, taking his place as one of the great men of the kingdom, litigating for his rights in the king's courts, building his castles, fighting his own and the king's wars, and seeking to establish and endow his dynasty. He is representative of a class, the medieval English baronage, at a time when its members were most secure and most assured. As we shall see (in chapter 12), his son lived on into more alarming times.

This does not mean that the life of every English baron of the thirteenth century was safe and uneventful. Apart from the ups and downs of court life or the occasional military expedition to France or Wales, the years 1258–65, the period of "baronial reform," saw the aristocracy split into factions and the crisis resolved only by pitched battles. Opposition to the government of Henry III became so strong that a set of constitutional limitations was placed on him in 1258. He spent several years seeking to evade or annul these restraints until, in 1264, recourse was had to war and the baronial opposition, headed by Simon de Montfort, defeated and captured the king at the battle of Lewes.

William de Briouze senior took the royalist side in this conflict, serving as a commander of the garrison defending Rochester Castle against de Montfort prior to Lewes, and as a consequence his lands were plundered by the family and adherents of de Montfort, while his son, William junior, was taken as a hostage. If William junior was correct in estimating his age at "about 46" in 1307, he was born c. 1260 and would thus have been only four years of age when taken into the de Montfort household as a guarantee for his father's good behavior. The account rolls of the household of Eleanor de Montfort, Simon's wife, survive for the year 1264–65, and show payments "for shoes for William de Briouze, 4½ pence," "for lining of squirrel fur for William de Briouze, 3 shillings and 4 pence." Even a few days before the decisive battle of Evesham (4 August 1265), at which Simon de Montfort was defeated and killed and his body dismembered, the accounts from his wife's household show payments to the servant looking after little William de Briouze. Aristocratic hostages might be more like houseguests than prisoners.

In the years following the battles of Lewes and Evesham, royal authority was slowly restored and William de Briouze junior grew from child to boy to young man. He is first recorded in the king's service in the 1280s, when he would have been in his twenties. Edward I spent two nights at the de Briouze castle of Oystermouth in the winter of 1284 and would certainly have met the young William de Briouze then, if not before. In April 1286, the year before the rebellion of Rhys ap Maredudd, William received royal letters of protection when "going beyond the seas in the king's service," which suggests he went with Edward I to Paris, where the English king did homage for his French lands to the new French king, Philip IV.

After he succeeded his father in 1291, William de Briouze continued loyally in the king's service. He contributed to Edward's wars in Wales, France, and Scotland both in person and by sending troops from his lordship of Gower. He was a regular participant in Edward's incessant Scottish campaigns, which began in 1296, and in 1297 he went with the king on the highly unpopular expedition to Flanders. As a reward he was granted the custody of John de Mowbray, minor heir of the deceased Baron Roger de Mowbray, whom he married off, at the age of eight, to his daughter Alina. Summoned regularly to parliament, he was one of the barons who put their seals to the defiant letter to Pope Boniface VIII in 1301 defending the rights of the Crown against papal intrusion.

Despite this record, he did on occasion clash with the king. Sometimes it seems to have been merely a matter of bad temper. In Michaelmas Term 1305, for instance, a lawsuit between William de Briouze junior and his stepmother Lady Mary, concerning a sum of eight hundred marks (a very large sum, well over £500) she was claiming from him, came before Roger de Higham, one of the king's most experienced judges. Roger and his colleagues decided in favor of Lady Mary. Immediately William de Briouze leapt over the bar of the court and began to rail against the judges. "Do you want to stand by this judgment?" he demanded of Roger de Higham, then shouted, "Roger, Roger, now you have what you have wanted for a long time." The judge asked, "And what is that?" "My shame and loss!" retorted de Briouze. "I will pay you back and put my mind to giving you my thanks for it." For this outburst against the royal judges William de Briouze was summoned before the king and his council. Forced to submit, he underwent a ritual humiliation, spending a night in the Tower of London and having to appear in the law courts, bareheaded and without a belt, to beg pardon from Roger de Higham.

Other issues between the king and the baron were more fundamental. The most important concerned the status of the de Briouze lordship of Gower and, in order to understand it, the special position of the Marcher lordships must first be appreciated. When, in the late eleventh and twelfth centuries, the Norman invaders created their conquest lordships in Wales, these territories were not annexed to the kingdom of England. They did not simply become part of England, with English law and administration. Yet, on the other hand, their lords were vassals of the king of England and recognized his authority. Hence their lordships were held from the king, even if they were not part of the kingdom.

As a consequence of this unusual situation, the balance between royal and lordly power was different in the Marcher lordships from that in most lordships in the kingdom of England. Notably, the Marcher lords claimed, and usually exercised, powers that would be regarded as royal within England. Although the king's ultimate judicial authority as feudal lord was recognized, his routine judicial power did not apply in the Marcher lordships—"the king's writ does not run," as the phrase went. While the writs that initiated lawsuits in England were obtained from the royal government, in the March they had to be sought from the chancery of the local lord. The lord claimed the right to determine all cases in his own court. Within their lordships the Marcher lords exercised "royal jurisdiction" (*jurisdictio regalis*).

The de Briouze family would be familiar with the claims inherent in Marcher status and with the clashes to which they sometimes led. In a particularly memorable incident in 1250, the Marcher Lord Walter Clifford was so incensed at receiving royal letters within his lordship that he forced the messenger to eat the letters, along with their wax seal. The story would have struck the de Brioiuzes not only because of the element of indigestibility but also because Walter Clifford was the second husband of John de Briouze's widow, hence the stepfather of William de Briouze senior.

Many years later, in 1281, William de Briouze senior was himself involved in a dispute that highlighted the essence of Marcher claims, as well as their contradictions. He had been on his way to his lordship of Gower and was passing through the neighboring Marcher lordship of Glamorgan, a possession of the earls of Gloucester, when one of the earl's officials blocked his way and prevented him from traveling along the highway. De Briouze took the case to the king's court but the earl responded that he had no obligation to answer the case there. "He has royal authority in Glamorgan," reads the report of his pleading, "and he and his predecessors have always been accustomed to hear all pleas." William de Briouze answered that he held his lands directly from the king and "seeks judgment if the earl ought to have jurisdiction concerning a trespass he himself had committed in the king's royal highway." The earl argued that he held his lands by conquest and should not be bound to answer the charge unless his fellow Marchers were consulted. The case dragged on for some time but reached no apparent resolution. It demonstrates, however, that de Briouze was willing enough to appeal to royal justice when injured by a fellow Marcher.

Edward I was a king determined to exercise his rights and, in order to do so, he had to know them. Soon after his coronation in 1274 proceedings were initiated to determine the basis on which lords claimed special privileges that were normally exercised by the Crown. Throughout England barons and lesser men possessed judicial and other rights, and the king's justices now made it their business to inquire if these rights were based on a grant by royal charter or simply on long custom. Findings were recorded in the so-called Hundred Rolls and individual cases subsequently pursued under the writ *quo warranto* ("by what warrant"). As an example we can take the rights exercised by William de Briouze in his main English lordship, Bramber in Sussex. In 1275 local juries reported that William de Briouze held all the hundreds of the Rape of Bramber. A "hundred" was an administrative subdivision of a county with its own court and minor judicial responsibilities, and many of them had been granted to the barons and great churches. The de Briouze stewards thus had the task of holding these courts and received the profits from them. Sometimes their conduct was a cause of grievance. The jurors of the hundred of Steyning complained that Thomas Merewe, steward of William de Briouze, had, in the year 1266–67, "put tenants who were free men on their oath at his own pleasure without the king's command, and this is a new custom contrary to the use of the country." Another de Briouze steward was accused of arresting suspected criminals and then taking bribes to release them. Apart from the holding of hundreds, other rights exercised by William de Briouze in the Rape of Bramber were "wreck of the sea, gallows, the assize of bread and ale, and other liberties which belong to the Crown." These entailed specifically the claim to anything cast upon the shore by the sea, especially from a wrecked ship; the right to hang a thief caught red-handed; and the prerogative of enforcing the legislation about the price of bread and ale.

Taken with his other rights, such as holding markets, levying tolls at the port of Shoreham, hearing disputes between his tenants, and so forth, this assemblage of privileges ("franchises") made William de Briouze the dominant nobleman in his part of Sussex. From his castle at Bramber, his estate administration extended throughout the Rape of which he was lord. Virtually all the claims he made—to his hundreds, right of wreck, gallows, and so on—were eventually accepted by Edward I. William's power was, however, always and everywhere under the supervision of the royal government, whose agents, the sheriff of Sussex and the royal judges, could and did establish limits to de Briouze authority and provide a superior, and vigilant, system of government.

The situation in the lordship of Gower was different. Here the de Briouzes had a chancery of their own, issuing writs that brought cases into their own court, the "county court" of Gower. They recognized no sheriffs or royal judges and expected to run Gower according to their own wishes, as tempered by local custom and opinion. They claimed "royal jurisdiction" like the other Marcher lords. When he sentenced William Cragh to be hanged, William de Briouze certainly did not expect to consult the king or his ministers. Yet even here, in the militarized borderlands far from Westminster, Edward I's government tested how far it could go, searching out limits and precedents, always pushing its most powerful card—the question "by what warrant?"

One thing that changed greatly after the annihilation of the native Welsh princes in the years 1277–82 was the extent of royal land in Wales. Previously there had been isolated royal strongholds at Carmarthen and Cardigan, plus lands of varying extent in the northeast of the country, but now there was a swath of royal lands stretching from Anglesey and Snowdonia in the north to Carmarthenshire in the south. It was the question of the size and jurisdiction of this last territory, the royal county of Carmarthen, that concerned the de Briouze lords of Gower. They sought to maintain the fullest interpretation of their rights as Marcher lords in the face of new, eager, and intrusive royal officials in southern Wales. Just as Rhys ap Maredudd had found the king's men difficult neighbors, so now the Marchers faced the same royalist pressure. The royal officials in southern and western Wales began to raise awkward questions about the rights of the lords of Gower.

The case was not a simple one between the king and William de Briouze, for it was generated partly by complaints brought by other parties against de Briouze. The bishop of Llandaff, who possessed the wealthy manor of Bishopston in Gower, objected to William de Briouze exercizing judicial authority over his tenants there—a manor which, the bishop claimed, "he held from the king and no other." This was a particularly vexed issue, for the king was insistent that the lands of the Welsh bishops were held from him and that the Marcher lords had no rights in them, especially no right to take them into their hands during a vacancy. The point had been established in regard to the bishopric of Llandaff in 1290, when William de Briouze senior had had to acknowledge the king's right.

Other de Briouze tenants joined the bishop in bringing complaints against William de Briouze before the king. Their very act of doing so entailed raising the issue of the Marcher status of Gower, for if, as William de Briouze claimed, he had "primary jurisdiction [*prima cognitio*] of all complaints and pleas within the land of Gower raised by his tenants," then these cases should be heard in his court at Swansea, not before the king's justices. The principle had to be clarified before the cases could proceed. Such situations, in which a lord's rights came under scrutiny when his tenants appealed to a superior lord, were a perennial feature of medieval law and politics. Indeed, the great political crises of the 1290s, the decade when the tenants of Gower first brought the legal status of the lordship into question, involved exactly this process. War broke out between the kings of England and France in 1294 because the king of France insisted on his "ex officio jurisdiction" (*cognitio ordinaria*) in the duchy of Gascony, which Edward I held as duke. One of the things that led to Edward's invasion of Scotland in 1296 was the quarrel over his rights as "superior lord" to hear appeals against the king of Scots from his Scottish vassals. Indeed, one of the ways that sovereignty was determined was by identifying ultimate judicial authority.

William de Briouze junior was an important baron and his case important enough to come before parliament, as it did in 1300, 1301, 1302, and 1305. In repeated hearings, the issues were debated and the two sides of the case elaborated. Walter of Pederton, a protégé of Robert de Tibetot and his successor as Justiciar of South Wales, argued that William de Briouze had usurped the rights he claimed, at the expense of the king and the royal county of Carmarthen. In response William produced the charter by which King John had granted Gower to his great-great-grandfather in 1203 (a copy of it also appears in the abbreviated Domesday Book that he commissioned at this time). Pederton retorted that the charter made no specific mention of "royal jurisdiction." During the pleadings at the Westminster parliament of July 1302, William de Briouze put his case as clearly as could be: "He ought to have his chancery and chancellor and seal, to serve his men of Gower when necessary; judgment of life and limb; and jurisdiction over all pleas, Crown pleas as well as others, within the land, as being part of the March and outside the county of Carmarthen and not within the power of its sheriff." The royal case was developed by the king's representative on this occasion, Nicholas of Warwick. The land of Gower, he asserted, had always been part of the county of Carmarthen until William de Briouze senior had, in the period after the battle of Evesham (1265), usurped royal jurisdiction "without warrant" (*absque warranto*), echoing the terms of *quo warranto*. King John's charter gave no justification for the exercise of such a privilege.

The king's council was persuaded by Nicholas of Warwick's case against William de Briouze, but the king "wished to deal more mildly with William" and ordered that inquiries should be held, both about the status of Gower and about the disputes between William and his men of Gower. At this time King Edward was well disposed toward William because of his "good service" in the Scottish wars. Indeed, in 1304, he even went so far as to grant him a charter that confirmed King John's grant of 1203 and conferred on him, as lord of Gower, the same liberties that the earl of Gloucester had in his Marcher lordship of Glamorgan. It might seem that this had settled the case, but objections were raised and yet further inquiries ordered. De Briouze's outburst against the royal judges in October 1305 may well have also created a more jaundiced view of his rights on the part of the king. In any event, in the winter of 1305–6 three royal judges, including the Justiciar of South Wales, Walter de Pederton, and Nicholas of Warwick, were ordered to go to Swansea in February 1306 to investigate the complaints of the men of Gower against William de Briouze and to hear evidence about the royal jurisdiction he claimed.

The sessions held at Swansea in February 1306, the year before William de Briouze gave his evidence at the canonization inquest, resolved the outstanding issues not by a judicial decision but by compromise. William de Briouze was forced to grant charters to his men of English Gower and to the burgesses of Swansea, promising them better lordship and abolishing what they saw as abuses (he made no promises to the inhabitants of Welsh Gower). The Crown, despite being able to muster a considerable body of evidence supporting its case, did not press the matter of "royal jurisdiction." In return for promising to rule in accordance with the terms of his charters of 1306 (one of them was later even called "the Magna Carta of Gower"), William de Briouze could continue to be a Marcher lord.

9

The Lady

L ess is known about Lady Mary de Briouze than about her
stepson. This is not an accident of the evidence but a fact
about the relative status of men and women. The bulk
of the written sources in the medieval period was generated by
institutions—the Church and secular government—that were
dominated by men, and most narrative and documentary texts
concerned areas of life—politics, warfare, landholding—where
men were in control. The result is that women are relatively invis-
ible in the written records. In the period covered here, the later
thirteenth and early fourteenth centuries, there are virtually no
private papers from aristocratic families and hence public records
form the greatest source of information on the lives of the aristocracy. The royal government was interested in William de Briouze,
senior and junior, as barons, warriors, counsellors, and landholders, and hence they crop up regularly in the records of the royal
administration. Lady Mary does not make an entry until her husband is dead and she becomes a landholder in her own right.

Even her ancestry is uncertain. It is known from the royal
records that she held the Manor of Weaverthorpe in the East
Riding of Yorkshire and that its superior lord at the time of her
death in 1326 was Sir William de Ros of Hamelak. Because this
manor has no connection with the other de Briouze estates and
is very distant from them, it has been assumed that it must have
been given to Lady Mary by her family as a marriage portion
(dowry) on the occasion of her marriage to William de Briouze.
If this assumption is right, then she would be a member of the

Yorkshire baronial family of de Ros, and probably, because of the relative ages involved, the daughter of Robert de Ros, who died in 1285. Although Robert de Ros and William de Briouze senior were on opposite sides in the baronial wars of 1264–65, Robert was pardoned by the king soon after the battle of Evesham. Their estates lay at a great distance from each other, but there would have been numerous occasions when the two barons would meet, in council and on campaign.

William de Briouze had much experience of matrimony. His first wife, Alina, mother of William junior, was in all likelihood also the daughter of a northern baronial family. After her death William senior married, and had a son by, the daughter of Nicholas de Moeles, who was custodian of the royal castles of Cardigan and Carmarthen in 1245 and would have then been a neighbor of the lord of Gower. Finally, probably around 1270, William took the Lady Mary as his third wife.

Lady Mary had several children by William de Briouze and her interest naturally lay in seeing that they acquired landed endowments that would allow them to live as aristocrats. Unless land were acquired through marriage or purchase, this could only be at the expense of their older half brothers. Provision was being made for Richard, her oldest son, in the 1280s, through the grant of the reversion of—that is, the right of succession to—various manors held by his father, William de Briouze senior; without such specific provision these would have gone to his oldest son, William junior. One of the richest of these manors was Tetbury in Gloucestershire, an outlying estate of the de Briouze family which must have formed a convenient stopping place in the endless journeys between their main lordships of Bramber and Gower. After the death of William de Briouze senior in 1291 (and some hard bargaining within the family) Tetbury went first to Richard, then, after his death in 1295, to his younger brother, Peter, and Peter's descendants. Providing for the children of a new bride could thus lead to a permanent diminution of the property of the main line. Daughters were less demanding and could be married off to neighboring nobles, as was Margaret, Lady Mary's daughter, who had lent a thread from her purse to measure William Cragh. She married Ralph de Camoys, an important landholder in Norfolk who also held the manor of Broadwater in the Rape of Bramber.

Lady Mary herself needed to be provided for in widowhood. English law at this time stipulated that a widow should receive a third of her husband's estate to support her after his death. This was known as dower. The dower lands involved could be specified while the husband was still alive or could be determined by negotiation after his death, which is what happened in the case of Lady Mary. By an agreement of March 1291 between William de Briouze junior and his stepmother, Lady Mary received for her lifetime the manors of Findon, Washington, Sedgewick, West Grinstead, Kingsbarns, and Beeding, in Sussex. These six manors were all situated in the southern part of the de Briouze Rape of Bramber. In addition, William de Briouze granted Lady Mary the use of the barn in the castle of Bramber to store her corn and gave her permission to live in the castle during the winter. She was to enjoy this substantial estate for the next thirty-five years, until her death in 1326. Since William de Briouze died a few weeks before his stepmother, he never regained possession of these dower lands. Such situations were not uncommon in aristocratic families and often led to bad feeling and litigation, even between biological sons and mothers, let alone stepsons and stepmothers.

From 1291 to 1326 Lady Mary was thus a wealthy widow with a solid landed base in Sussex. Her estates in that county were valued at over £130 per annum, and this does not take into account her various properties elsewhere, for, in addition to Weaverthorpe in Yorkshire, she had lands granted to her for life by her own sons. Her main manor house seems to have been at Findon, where Edward I visited her in the summer of 1305 (she seized the chance to procure a royal writ in favor of her son Peter). The rector of Findon, at least by 1307, was William of Codineston. He enjoyed a wealthy parish, for Findon was valued at £26 13s. 4d. in the ecclesiastical tax assessment of 1291. Even given deductions to support a vicar (who would do most of the work), this gave William of Codineston an income equivalent to that of a country gentleman. Lady Mary was thus a great lady with a family chaplain of independent means. There is no record of her ever having been sought in marriage again, despite the property she would have brought with her.

She figures in the records of the time mainly as a party to litigation. This is unsurprising for two reasons: first, the bulk of the surviving documents from this period come from the royal government and law courts; second, landed aristocrats did engage in continual litigation. Their standing was based primarily on their landed property and hence it had to be protected, and if possible enlarged, at all costs. The elaboration of the English legal system in the century or so before the reign of Edward I meant that there were countless legal devices to deploy in raising claims and rebutting them, and a new class of professional lawyers made a living from the land disputes of the aristocracy. Litigation over land was a relatively safe activity and could be rewarding. Moreover, agreements recorded in the law courts were the most secure way to ensure even amicable family settlements, so these often came before the judges too.

Lady Mary and William de Briouze junior were involved in litigation over her dower as early as 1292, the year following their agreement about the Sussex manors. One case concerned the manor of Wickhambreux in Kent (the name means "Wickham of the de Briouze"), a third of which Mary claimed as dower. Other disputes turned on the question of the debts and chattels of William de Briouze senior, Lady Mary claiming almost £400 from her husband's Welsh lands and about £90 from his English estates. Her stepson promised to deliver a full accounting at Horsham, one of his Sussex manors adjoining Lady Mary's. One aspect of the consequent transactions reveals the complexities of a Marcher lord's situation. At the time of his death William de Briouze senior had been owed eight hundred marks (over £500) by his Welsh tenants for a fine (this term could mean payment for an agreement as well as a penalty). William de Briouze junior agreed, as part of his settlement with his stepmother, to raise this money and to use it, to pay off her debts to the Crown. To get help in levying the money from the Welsh, he requested a "writ of aid" under the Exchequer seal. This was in November 1292. Less than a year later, however, in September 1293, William was denying that Exchequer writs had ever been answered to in the Welsh Marcher lordships. He wanted the king's help from time to time but he hoped to have it on his own terms (this sum of eight hundred marks was the subject of the litigation of 1305, mentioned in chapter 8, when William de Briouze jumped over the bar of the court to insult the judges).

Lady Mary's sons, Richard and Peter, entered the royal service and served together in Wales in 1295, helping suppress the Welsh rebellion of that year. Soon afterwards, on 27 September 1295, Richard died at Canterbury and was buried under a cloth provided by Edward I himself. Peter inherited Tetbury and some other property and was well enough provided for. Lady Mary's daughter, Margaret, was married to Ralph de Camoys by 1303 and Lady Mary ensured that her daughter and son-in-law would succeed to her manor of Little Bookham in Surrey by granting it to them and then receiving it back from them for life. Every such family arrangement was likely to come to the law courts and this was no exception. In the first week of June 1307 the chief justice of the bench, Ralph of Hengham, heard a case between Lady Mary, on the one part, and Ralph de Camoys and Margaret, on the other. Although Lady Mary had granted Little Bookham to them by charter, others had raised claims to the manor. Lady Mary was summoned to "warrant" her grant; that is, to defend it against the other claimants in place of Ralph and Margaret. She admitted that she owed warranty and promised that, if she failed to ensure their possession of the manor, she would compensate them from her estate of Weaverthorpe in Yorkshire. The case itself is fairly routine but it does show one of the reasons that Lady Mary might be a regular visitor to Westminster. Her testimony at the canonization hearings, which was heard in London on 14 July 1307, just five weeks after the case involving Little Bookham, was given, according to the record, when "she had come to the city of London for other reasons." Perhaps litigation was one of them. Curiously enough the very first witness in the canonization inquiry, testifying immediately before Lady Mary, was Chief Justice Ralph of Hengham.

When Lady Mary had given her testimony about William Cragh in London in 1307, the commissioners observed, "because this lady was not experienced in law and legal proceedings and much of her evidence was hearsay and she was brought forth as a witness only for this one miracle, the commissioners declined to interrogate her further." The element of condescension in these comments is clear; the commissioners obviously underestimated Lady Mary's experience in lawsuits. Even though by this period most of the actual pleading in English law courts would be conducted not by the parties but by their legal representatives, Lady Mary was in fact a veteran of litigation. Her experience was of English Common Law, not of the Romano-canonical procedures favored by the papal commission, and hence the course followed by the inquiry might be unfamiliar, but she was not an innocent abroad. Despite the commissioners' condescending comment and although Lady Mary was the only female witness interrogated about the case of William Cragh, there is no other evidence that she was treated differently and her testimony reveals no distinctive features that could plausibly be connected with her sex. This may, of course, be an illusion. Both the standard set of questions that the commissioners used and the ecclesiastical Latin into which all testimony was translated have the effect of flattening and rendering more uniform the individual oral statements of the witnesses. In any case, Lady Mary is certainly the only one of the nine witnesses in the case to be dismissed with a belittling remark in the record.

One of the largest uncertainties in the whole story of the death and resurrection of William Cragh is why Lady Mary interceded for him in the first place. If this book were a novel or a film, it would be easy to write in a previous love interest, an earlier romantic meeting between the highborn lady and the wild Welsh rebel. However, since this is a work of dry objective history, that possibility is debarred. It may be some comfort to recognize that the witnesses in the case had no more certain ground than we do in explaining her role. Most of them do not refer to her motives at all, and John of Baggeham, who received her instructions about the case in person, reported blankly, "Lady Mary had sought the body of this William, he did not know why." Her central role was, nevertheless, recognized. Adam of Loughor mentioned that it was common talk that William Cragh had been "measured to God and Saint Thomas de Cantilupe at the command of the lady of the castle" and Henry Skinner gave a very similar report. William Cragh himself had heard people say that "the lady of the castle" had asked her husband that his body should be granted to her, so that it could be buried in the churchyard, while William de Briouze junior, as we have seen (in chapter 1), reported Lady Mary's very words: "Let us pray to God and Saint Thomas de Cantilupe that he give him life and, if he give him life, we will conduct him to Saint Thomas."

The most remarkable testimony on this subject is that of William of Codineston, the de Briouze family chaplain. He had indeed heard tell that William Cragh had been "measured to Saint Thomas de Cantilupe" but "he did not know by whom or at whose instigation." This is astonishing. William was an intimate member of the de Briouze household; was present, by his own account, when William Cragh had been summoned before the lord and the lady in the castle chamber; he was rector of the parish where Lady Mary spent her widowhood; and yet in his testimony before the commissioners in 1307 he said he did know who had advocated putting the case of William Cragh in the hands of Saint Thomas de Cantilupe. Contact between the manor house and the rectory at Findon must have been less personal than we might imagine.

It is clearly significant that it was a lady who interceded for the condemned Welshman, for intercession was a traditional role of highborn women in the medieval period. They were pictured as more approachable than their stern husbands, and entreaties and requests might be made to and through them. An instance that dates to only a few years earlier than the hanging of William Cragh is the approach made by John Pecham, archbishop of Can-

terbury (1279–92), to Eleanor of Castile, queen of England and
wife of Edward I, on behalf of the bishop of Winchester, who
was out of royal favor:

> My lady, the saints teach us that women are by nature more pitiful
> and more devout than men. This is why Scripture says "where there
> is no wife, he that is in want mourns." And because God has given
> you greater honor than all others within your lordship, it is right that
> your pity should surpass the pity of all men and women within your
> lordship. Wherefore we beseech you, by God and Our Lady, that you
> make the heart of our lord king favorable to our dear brother, the
> bishop of Winchester.

There is a complex network of intercession here. The archbishop
invokes God and the Virgin Mary ("Our Lady") to help in his
request to the queen ("my lady") to intercede with her husband
on behalf of the bishop. Queen Eleanor may in reality have been
a hard and grasping woman, "widely notorious for her land hunger," but in this letter she appears in a conventional guise, as a
compassionate lady able to sway her husband's heart.

Queen Eleanor died on Saturday, 25 November 1290, the day
before William Cragh was condemned to be hanged. She had
done her duty by Edward, producing thirteen children before her
death at the age of forty-four, and the king's grief was expressed
in the erection of "Eleanor's Crosses" at the resting places of her
funeral bier, the most well known today being Charing Cross. As
her funeral cortege made its way to Westminster, William Cragh
was condemned, hanged, and revived. It is entirely plausible that
the sentiment Archbishop Pecham had expressed to queen Eleanor—"because God has given you greater honor than all others
within your lordship, it is right that your pity should surpass the
pity of all men and women within your lordship"—was present
in the mind of Lady Mary de Briouze when she made her plea
to her husband to save the hanged man. She too stood in an
intercessory position between a lord with the power of life and
death and his subjects and potential victims. Her account of her
intervention, as recounted during the canonization hearings, is
bald and without any hint of motive: "Before William and the

other man were hanged, the lady had asked her husband to spare the two robbers and to give them to her, and her husband refused this to her." Despite her repeated requests, William de Briouze senior resisted, until William Cragh was dead. Then he gave him to his wife "such as he was."

At the time of the incident William de Briouze senior was about seventy years of age, while his wife was certainly younger, possibly by as much as thirty years. Their power struggle over the fate of William Cragh was between an old, experienced, battle-hardened baron of the Welsh March and his younger wife, brought to the region only by her marriage. As we know from the testimony of John of Baggeham, the head of the execution squad, there were men who thought it a very bad thing to revive William Cragh. The younger, alien "lady of the castle" may have been exhibiting "pity surpassing the pity of all men and women within her lordship" but she could make no headway against the decisions of the male ruler of that lordship. Only after the death of William Cragh did she find a more responsive lord. "Let us pray to God and Saint Thomas de Cantilupe that he give him life," she had said, finally finding an intercessor who would give her what she wanted.

Narrative, Memory, and Inquisition

At the end of the record of the canonization process are the names of four notaries involved in recording it: Raymond de la Prada; Adam, son of Adam Swayny, of Butterwick, called "of Lindsey," from the diocese of Lincoln; William, son of William le Dorturer of Selborne, from the diocese of Winchester; and Ranulf Daniel of Waltham Holy Cross, from the diocese of London.

Notaries received their authority, technically, from either the pope or the Holy Roman Emperor, or from those with power delegated by them. Raymond de la Prada describes himself as "public notary by imperial authority and by the authority of the Reverend Father Lord William, by grace of God, bishop of Mende." The three others also describe themselves as public notaries, Adam and William by papal and imperial authority and by the authority of the prefect of Rome, Ranulf solely "by the authority of the Holy Roman Empire."

Notaries were scribes authorized to produce official records that would be deemed authoritative in a law court. They authenticated their texts not by a wax seal, which was the customary form in England, but by an elaborate "sign manual," a complex, even baroque mark in ink, made up of curls, curves, and, sometimes, stylized drawings of objects. It would be very hard to imitate and, in the history of the development of documentary authentication, occupies a place between the seal and the signature of modern times. The signs manual of Raymond, Adam, William, and Ranulf, the four notaries involved in recording the canonization process, can be found in the manuscript record of the inquest.

The profession of public notary was relatively new in England. Foreign notaries had been active in the kingdom since the late 1250s but it was only with the pontificate of John Pecham, archbishop of Canterbury, whose letter to Queen Eleanor is cited above (in chapter 9), that notarial activity in general and the appointment of English notaries in particular became common. Immediately after his consecration Pecham received papal authorization to appoint three notaries, and by the time of his death in 1292 notaries were active in more than half the dioceses of England. Adam of Lindsey is first mentioned as a notary in 1289, eighteen years before the canonization process of Thomas de Cantilupe, so he was not only an enormously experienced man when employed by the papal commissioners in 1307 but he was also one of the pioneer generation of the notarial profession in England.

The duty of the notaries present at the hearings of the commission was to make a record of the proceedings, recording both the interrogation of the witnesses and such details as the terms of the questionnaire governing the examination, the date and place of the hearings, and the names of those present. As explained in chapter 3 everything said had to be translated into Latin, and the commission relied on the assistance of English-speaking friars for this purpose (as well as the unusual case of the Welsh-speaking friars when William Cragh was interrogated). Of the nine witnesses in the Cragh case five testified in French, three in English and one in Welsh. Not surprisingly, the French speakers included the aristocratic Mary and William de Briouze; their chaplain, the wealthy clergyman William of Codineston; and the steward of their household in Gower, John of Baggeham. Thomas Marshall, although a poor priest, also gave his evidence in French. The other inhabitants of Swansea, Henry Skinner, a propertied man; Adam of Loughor, a craftsman; and John ap Hywel, a hired laborer, spoke in English (despite the Welsh descent that is obvious from John's name). The testimony of Thomas Marshall and Henry Skinner suggests that they could understand some Welsh, implying that competence in the language of the conquered was more likely to be found among the educated and better-off of the conquerors than among the lower-class settlers.

Not only were the words of the witnesses subject to the filter of translation, being transformed from first person to third person in the process, they were also sifted through the unyielding sieve of the commissioners' questionnaire. The twenty-five questions it contained structured a witness's testimony and set boundaries to it. Those giving evidence were not expected to tell their story as they saw fit but to respond to prompts. Moreover, not only did the inquisitorial framework force their recollections into predefined channels, it also required them to give answers on issues about which they might never otherwise have reflected. Two prominent examples are the extent of public knowledge of the miraculous revival of William Cragh and the question of whether it was a natural or supernatural occurrence.

Public knowledge (*fama*) is a recurrent issue for the commissioners, and questions twelve and thirteen of section three of the questionnaire inquired "if the miracles were publicized" and "if there is and was public knowledge of the miracles." They wanted to know the extent of Thomas de Cantilupe's renown because a widespread reputation as a saint could be supporting ground for canonization. Far from it being the case that Catholics were forbidden to regard someone as a saint until he or she had been officially canonized, a decision to canonize was made more likely by the fact that the candidate already had an extensive cult. To be regarded as a saint was an argument for one's sanctity.

The witnesses responded positively, but quite generally, to the question about public reputation. William de Briouze testified that "it was public knowledge and general report in the region, and still is, and everybody speaking together about this believes and asserts, that William Cragh was resuscitated miraculously and through the merits of Saint Thomas de Cantilupe." Lady Mary said that the events she had described "had been and still are common report and the common opinion of people and public knowledge in Gower and Hereford." Both she and William Cragh mention the specific publicity given to the miracle during the thanksgiving visit to Hereford, with the ringing of bells and the singing of the *Te Deum*, traditional expressions of rejoicing when miracles were reported.

Sometimes it is possible to detect a hint of a leading question. William Cragh's interrogation, for example, includes the following exchange: "Asked if, in his country after the time of his hanging, it was publicly and commonly ascribed, and still is ascribed, to a miracle performed by the merits of the Lord Saint Thomas that he obtained and recovered life after the hanging, he answered 'yes.'" It is perhaps hard to imagine his answering "no" to a question phrased in this way. Yet, in general, the commissioners were very far from engineering simple responses favorable to the canonization. They raised objections, pursued follow-up questions and asked the witnesses to clarify their terms. In exchanges over the issue of public knowledge this technique is especially explicit. After William of Codineston had reported that the whole incident was "public knowledge" in Swansea at the time that it happened, the commissioners, trained in the analytical and definitional techniques of high scholasticism, and perhaps presuming that this well-off priest shared their education, or should at least be reminded of it, responded with the question, "What did he call 'public knowledge'?" William of Codineston did the best he could: public knowledge was "what is said in many places publicly and is publicized commonly among everyone." This perfectly acceptable, if anodyne, definition seems to have satisfied the questioners, for they moved on to ask if the matter were still public knowledge in Swansea. William did not know, "for he had not been there since."

But it was not only clergymen who were subject to this tutorial cross-examination. William de Briouze himself had to attempt clarifications and definitions. After his statement quoted above, that the miracle was "public knowledge," he was asked the source of his knowledge. "He had heard it," he said, "publicly related in this way by all who talked about the matter and he heard nothing contrary said by anyone." Like his chaplain, the baron was then called upon to attempt a definition: "What did he call 'public knowledge' and what did he believe it to be?" He interpreted it as "something . . . so true that people commonly assert publicly that it is so and no one says the opposite, nor does it appear to be otherwise." This, he added, was the situation in the case at hand.

It may be natural to regard these circular and possibly bemused attempts at definition as simply vacuous dead ends in the interrogation, but they do underline certain of its important features. The inquest was carried out by men trained in sophisticated techniques of intellectual analysis. They were very concerned with the reputation of the candidate for sanctity. Moreover, "public knowledge" or "public reputation" (*fama*) was not a rarified concept found only in the lecture room but had an important place in most systems of medieval law, in customary and secular law as well as in the more academic Roman and canon law. It could be important in deciding whether a marriage was valid; its weight could be crucial in heresy trials; and one of the most frequent ways in which criminal charges were brought in England was through "presentment," when a grand jury reported that an individual was generally believed to be guilty of an offence. It was the "public reputation" of being involved in the crime that brought the name of the suspect before the judges. The respondents in the inquest into the canonization of Thomas de Cantilupe would thus know that there were important social, pragmatic, and legal implications connected with the level of the public knowledge of the miracle.

Another issue in which the commissioners' training as analytical thinkers appears is the question of whether the revival of the hanged man could have been natural. By this period scholastic thinking had developed complex positions about which features made events "natural" or "supernatural" (the latter term indeed being an invention of thirteenth-century theologians and philos-

ophers). The inquisitors knew that if the resuscitation had been
a natural event it could not have been a miracle and hence could
not be used to support Thomas de Cantilupe's canonization.
Asked directly if the incident had been "above or contrary to
nature," William de Briouze replied that he did not believe William Cragh could have escaped death "through the powers or
force of human nature." This is not literally the same as saying
the event was "above or contrary to nature," even if compatible
with it, and perhaps we are hearing two different idioms, one the
expression of the university educated clergy, the other a more
commonplace language of "human nature." William of Codineston was more succinct, answering the question in the affirmative
and adding that the hanged man "could not have avoided death
without a miracle." Lady Mary's answer was the fullest. Asked if
William Cragh could have survived "according to nature and the
course of nature without a divine miracle," she relied emphati-
cally that "she did not believe, nor did she know of and had not
heard anyone saying, that he could have lived without a divine
miracle above nature."

The hearings thus constituted a genuine interrogation, with
the commissioners positively grilling the witnesses. The witnesses' responses to incidental and supplementary questions are
sometimes visible in the text. Many of these are negative—"he
answered he did not remember," "he said he did not know," "she
did not know at what time"—and the record of these proceedings
thus provides not only evidence of what was remembered or
known but also of what was not. An instance has already been
mentioned above (in chapter 9), in the discussion of William
of Codineston's remarkable ignorance of who was behind the
"measuring" of William Cragh. Another illuminating aspect of
the hearings is who knows whose names. William de Briouze,
for instance, stated explicitly, when asked, that he did not know
the name of the burgess to whose house the apparent corpse of
William Cragh was carried, while he was also ignorant of William Cragh's parentage or place of origin (more specifically than
Gower). In contrast, all six witnesses from Swansea, with the
exception of Henry Skinner, who had not gone to see the corpse,

mention the name of Thomas Mathews as the householder. Their knowledge of local society was clearly greater than that of the lord of Swansea. They are less unanimous about William Cragh's background, some not knowing his parentage or parish, while others are able to identify his kin precisely.

It is always tempting to speculate on the reasons for certain things being known or remembered, certain things forgotten. For instance, when we consider that Lady Mary de Briouze, interrogated in 1307, could not remember whether Sunehild, the lady-in-waiting whom she sent to measure William Cragh in 1290, was still alive nor where she might be, but that William de Briouze junior could, and knew that Sunehild was now dead, we might wonder about this. Is it possible, we might ask, that his more sharply focused attention on his stepmother's female attendants had a romantic or erotic basis? The case is, however, an instructive warning that our speculations may lead us astray. The records of the proceedings before the royal justices in Gower in 1306 reveal that a "Sunehild of Swansea" had once sued William de Briouze in order to claim a family property that she alleged William had taken from her. If this is the same woman as Lady Mary's attendant, which is very likely, then conflict over property rather than old and secret longings appears to have been the reason that the lord was so well informed about Sunehild.

Lady Mary's ignorance of the fortunes of her lady-in-waiting can also be explained by the fact that she had, in all probability, never returned to Gower after leaving it on the journey of thanksgiving after William Cragh's resurrection. After her husband's death in January 1291, Lady Mary was given as her dower de Briouze estates located entirely in southern England. She had no share in the Gower lordship and, if she had any desire to see her stepson, this could be fulfilled when he visited his Sussex estates, although, since the two were engaged in perennial litigation, they may not even have sought each other's company. Hence she never returned to the scene of the miracle. The same is true of another witness, William of Codineston who, by 1307, was rector of Findon. It is not certain when he acquired the benefice but as soon as he did he had a firm basis in a secure and comfortable position in one of Lady Mary's dower manors. He states explicitly that after 1290 he had never again visited the Welsh lordship where William Cragh was hanged. All baronial families had scattered estates, but the de Briouze holdings were unusual in having two concentrated nuclei, Bramber and Gower, at a great distance from each other. Even the de Briouze dowager and the family chaplain could go for decades without visiting the Gower part of the estate.

Lady Mary and William of Codineston were thus in a different category from the other witnesses, all of whom had maintained strong links with Gower and Swansea in the years between the miracle and the inquiry. Indeed, in the case of all except William de Briouze himself, they had probably resided there continuously. This is extremely relevant to the question of recall. If subsequent discussion of an incident takes place, that incident is more firmly lodged in the memory, even if it may be reshaped in the process. The Swansea witnesses had the opportunity—even if they did not take it—to develop their recall by sharing impressions, while Lady Mary and the parish priest had been removed from the scene as if by helicopter and had evidently not nursed each other's memories since. John of Baggeham probably saw the castle and the site of the gallows every day; Lady Mary had not seen or heard of her local female attendants for many years. The testimony of the nine witnesses thus does not give rise to nine strands of equal weight and independence. This is not to say that the six Swansea witnesses represent a friendly social group, without mutual rancor and contempt. One of them at least, John of Baggeham, head of the execution squad, thought that another, William Cragh, should have been dead. Not only that, but at the end of his testimony John felt that he had to volunteer the shameful fact that John ap Hywel "does not have property from the revenue of which he can live, but he lives by his own labor." Even William Cragh seems to have been sensitive to economic standing. When he was asked if he knew the other witnesses, he replied that he did and that they were generally regarded as men who were trustworthy, free, and with sufficient property to live on, "except for Sir Thomas the priest, who had no benefice" (the "sir" here is simply a complimentary title bestowed upon all priests).

It has already been pointed out (in chapter 6) that some of the Swansea witnesses had traveled together to Hereford to give their evidence and had discussed the case on the way. It is not entirely clear how much other contact there had been in the years between the miracle in 1290 and the depositions in 1307. A memory frequently prompted and explored in company with others is a very different thing from a memory evoked by carefully structured questioning after a period of seventeen years. If the miracle were indeed the subject of widespread public discussion both when it occurred and afterwards, as many of the witnesses reported, then it obviously continued to be a regularly recounted story. When the Hereford Cathedral clergy were looking for witnesses to support the canonization of their bishop, they would seek out those people who were indicated to them as useful sources of information and one would expect such people to be those who had a local reputation for telling the tale. Hence the likelihood is that the witnesses from Swansea were not dredging their memory for the first time when they came before the commissioners. In the case of William Cragh and John of Baggeham, the hanged man and the head of the execution squad, it is hard to believe each had not told his story dozens of times before.

Memory can be long or short, clear or hazy. In some areas of medieval life very long memories were cultivated. For instance, in 1278 the earl of Warwick raised a claim to the lordship of Gower against William de Briouze senior. The earls of Warwick had ruled Gower in the twelfth century but lost control of it, apparently selling it to the king before 1184. The lawsuit of 1278 thus looked back ninety-four years. Nobles may not have known the exact year of their birth but they nursed long memories of their estates, particularly those they had lost (the claim was unsuccessful at the time but was revived in 1354, 170 years after the earls had forfeited possession). Naturally, written records as well as family lore played a part in the transmission of such ancient claims. Genealogical memory was obviously important in a dynastic society in which power was based primarily on the inheritance of land, but its length and breadth varied. The Welsh were renowned for their genealogical knowledge and pride, and lengthy genealogies were transmitted both orally and in writing. William de Briouze, as we have seen (in chapter 8) was able to look up the holdings of his distant ancestor that were recorded in Domesday Book, over two centuries earlier. Yet outside such practical matters his genealogical awareness became vague. When asked the standard question put by the commissioners as to whether he was related to Thomas de Cantilupe, William de Briouze replied that he believed so, "in the third or fourth grade," but was not certain. Modern historians know that William de Briouze and Thomas de Cantilupe were, in fact, distantly related by marriage, the saint's brother having married Eve de Briouze, the second cousin of William de Briouze senior, but this wider family perspective was not especially sharp in the mind of William de Briouze. Given a combination of a practical economic purpose and the existence of written record, he could look back two hundred years with clarity; he did not, however, live in a world that was always more memorious than our own.

The depositions of the nine witnesses to the resurrection of William Cragh constitute neither one story nor nine stories. They are not unconstrained narratives of a strange event but answers given on oath and shaped by a set of procedures and assumptions that were brought to the task by highly trained men, men who came from a world rather different from that of the witnesses. The closest similarities of education and outlook between commissioners and witnesses would probably be those between the English clergymen Bishop Ralph Baldock and William of Codineston, but even here a wide gap in culture and experience existed. The testimony in this case (like that of the two hundred other witnesses in the canonization process) was elicited for a purpose, to judge the personal merits and supernatural powers of a bishop who had died twenty-five years earlier. In many ways this purpose shapes the narratives, because the narratives were shaped by the commissioners' predetermined questions. Yet, as we have also seen, despite the constraining network of the procedure—or sometimes because of it—light is shed on many and varied aspects of the physical and mental world of the late thirteenth and early fourteenth centuries.

The New Saint

W hen Lady Mary de Briouze, having failed to win the ear of her husband in the case of William Cragh, turned for help to Thomas de Cantilupe, the dead bishop's reputation for miracles was relatively recent. Cantilupe died on 25 August 1282, but miracles began only four and a half years later, at Eastertide 1287, when his successor, Bishop Richard Swinfield, moved his remains to a new tomb in Hereford Cathedral. This immediately stimulated a wave of miraculous cures. The blind saw, the lame walked, and news of the remarkable events spread outwards in a wave from Hereford. The monastic annalist at nearby Worcester recorded this as the time, "when God first showed to the world the sanctity of Thomas de Cantilupe through manifest miracles."

Bishop Swinfield's action in moving Cantilupe's remains was not casual. The translation (ritual relocation) of a body was an ancient and traditional method of marking the sanctity of the individual concerned. Indeed, for many centuries, before the popes asserted their own monopoly of the power to canonize, translation was the virtual equivalent of canonization. Naturally, there would be other reasons for moving bodies and tombs, but a grand ceremonial relocation of the type undertaken by Swinfield at the high point of the Christian year suggested that the bones being elevated were those of a saint. That this is how the ceremony was understood is clear from the response of the local people who found healing at the tomb. Swinfield, who had been Cantilupe's chaplain for many years, was obviously one of the major forces behind his cult. Early in his episcopate he issued instructions that inquiries should be made as to whether any miracles were occurring at the place in Italy where Cantilupe's flesh had been buried (his bones had been brought back to England after the flesh had been boiled off). He also commanded that "inquiries should be made by the dean and other discreet men as to what the pope thinks about the bishop and the miracles performed through him, and this should all be reported in writing, and whether it is expedient to seek canonization, and how and in what way." A campaign was being planned and the ceremony at Easter 1287 was a public statement of it.

In the following years Cantilupe's new tomb became the focus of a pilgrim cult, with hundreds of visitors from an ever widening area. By the early 1290s offerings at the shrine brought in over £200 per annum, the equivalent of a baronial income, while the wax tapers placed there were so numerous that the dean and treasurer of the cathedral became embroiled in a dispute over who should have them. It is not surprising that Lady Mary de Briouze could claim that, in the year 1290, she had a special devotion to the saint. Briouze connections with Hereford were extensive; although it had been many years since a family member had actually been bishop of Hereford (this was Giles de Briouze, William senior's great-uncle, who died in 1215), the deaths of various members of the family were recorded in the cathedral obit book, which listed those who should be commemorated. Hugh de Briouze, who was penitentiary of the diocese of Hereford from 1293 to 1320, during the vital period of the canonization campaign, is known to have been illegitimate, although his links with the legitimate de Briouzes is not clear (chronologically he could have been an illegitimate son of William de Briouze senior).

By the time he was invoked to save William Cragh, in November 1290, Thomas de Cantilupe had already been proposed to the pope for official canonization. A letter from Bishop Swinfield, dated 19 April 1290, told the pope of his numerous miracles, which were widely reported throughout England and beyond. He was, Swinfield wrote, more confident in asserting the bishop's sanctity because he had been a member of his household for eighteen years and had seen at first hand his virtue, piety, and auster-ity. He humbly begged the pope to inscribe Thomas de Cantilupe in the catalog of the saints, placing him, "a flaming and glowing light, attested by many miracles" on the "candlestick of the Church."

A period of more than sixteen years passed between Swin-field's letter requesting canonization and the authorization of the canonization inquiry by Clement V on 23 August 1306. Some of the delay could be due to the changing circumstances of the pa-pacy. The letter of 1290 was sent to Nicholas IV, who died in April 1292, two years later, and there then followed a vacancy of over two years before the improbable election of the eighty-five-year-old hermit Celestine V. Resigning after fewer than six months, he was replaced, in December 1294, by the ambitious and autocratic Boniface VIII, whose reign was marked by inter-mittent conflict with the lay powers, culminating in his seizure and mistreatment by agents of the king of France. His successor, Benedict XI, was pope for less than a year (1303–4), whereupon there was an eleventh-month vacancy before the election of Clement V. With a history such as this, a consistent papal policy on the canonization of Thomas de Cantilupe might be hard to maintain.

Throughout these years Bishop Swinfield maintained the pressure. He enlisted the aid of his fellow bishops, who were encouraged to write to the pope using form letters supplied by Swinfield. A typical one is that sent by Oliver Sutton, bishop of Lincoln, in 1294: "Since the Lord has deigned to perform many miracles through Lord Thomas de Cantilupe of happy memory, once bishop of Hereford, whose bones rest in the church of Here-ford, as is attested by public reputation throughout the kingdom of England, I inform your holiness of this so that my testimony may help the favourable outcome of the petition for his canoniza-tion." Clusters of such letters were sent in 1294, 1299, and 1305. In addition, the dean and chapter of Hereford appointed a repre-sentative at the papal court especially charged with procuring the canonization, although the relationship was marred by disputes over expenses.

Swinfield not only mobilized the bishops but was also able to secure the backing of the king himself. Edward I had known Cantilupe personally, for he had served on the royal council, and was now eager, as he put it, "to have as a sympathetic patron in heaven him whom we had in our household on earth." The election of Clement V in the summer of 1305 prompted a spate of letters from king and bishops to the new pope and to the cardinals pressing for the canonization. As we have seen, this renewed barrage proved effective. In August 1306 the commission was established and by the summer of the following year Lady Mary, William de Briouze, and William of Codineston were giving their testimony.

The collection of the testimony by William Durand, Ralph Baldock, and William de Testa was a laborious process. It was also an expensive one—the Hereford cathedral archives still contain such items as William de Testa's receipt for £20 for his expenses that he issued to the canons, and a similar acknowledgment for £3 paid out to a notary "in the process of inquiry on the miracles performed by Lord Thomas de Cantilupe." The writing out of the proceedings of the inquiry and the transmission of the report to the papal court were not, of course, the end of the matter. The findings needed to be sifted and assessed before a final decision was made. This took time and was subject to the same kind of delays as had preceded the establishment of the commission.

The time from Cantilupe's death to his canonization was thirty-eight years, a rather long period for a thirteenth-century saint (although Thomas Aquinas required longer, forty-nine years). Some of the reasons for the slow progress of canonizations can be gathered from a revealing, but incomplete, account of the scrutiny given to the documents in the case once they reached Avignon. In May 1313 Clement V instructed a group of cardinals to examine the report of the canonization inquest of 1307. The gap of five and a half years is probably to be explained by the pope's preoccupation with suppressing the Templars, moving to Avignon, and holding the Council of Vienne. In the meantime the new king of England, Edward II, had continued to support the case, sending letters to pope and cardinals, instructing his agent Adam of Orleton to follow up the commissioners' reports, and even securing the help of Philip IV of France, who put in a good word at the Council of Vienne.

The first thing the cardinals did in 1313 was to produce an inventory of the documents. This formidable list contains over twenty items, some of them multiple, and includes letters from the kings of England and France and from the English bishops and barons, a copy of Pope Clement's letter announcing the inquiry, the volumes containing the inquiry into Cantilupe's excommunication (discussed in chapter 3), and the volume with the results of the canonization inquest, now safely in the papal court. Cardinal Berengar, who presided over this committee of cardinals, had the items listed by two notaries. Then, on 14 May 1313, the cardinals, along with the notaries, assembled in Berengar's house in Avignon and began the examination of this little archive. Starting with the report of the inquiry into Cantilupe's excommunication, they read through the first thirty pages. Next day they continued, reaching page fifty-six . They agreed to meet next day to continue their work; here, unfortunately, the account of these proceedings breaks off. However, since the record of the inquiry into the excommunication still exists, it is possible to calculate that, at this rate, they would have needed a total of ten days to read through the excommunication inquiry and more than three weeks to deal with the canonization process. The mere examination of the documents thus required well over a month of full-time work. Since cardinals were busy men, with many calls on their time, it is not surprising that the canonization proceeded at a slow pace.

One of the most fascinating documents to have survived from the canonization process is the record of the deliberations on Cantilupe's miracles made by an anonymous analyst at the papal court at some time between 1318 and 1320. His task was to abstract the essential details of the miracles, subject them to critical scrutiny, and jot down his observations. All possible scruples about the accounts given to the papal commissioners in 1307 would be raised, all improbabilities and contradictions noted. Sadly, the resurrection of William Cragh was not one of the miracles commented upon, but there is a long discussion of the case of Roger of Conway, a little boy saved from a fall into the moat of Conway Castle and adopted by Bishop Ralph Baldock (discussed in chapter 12):

> Doubt may arise about how the tender body of the boy falling onto a stone surface from such a height was not completely shattered. Let it be said that although it was tender it was nevertheless of less weight than the body of a full-grown man and, being of less weight, the shattering would be less and the impact less when he fell onto rock or earth, and also the way he fell might have led to less shattering of the body. For if in falling the limbs and legs are kept as still as a stone, the impact of a falling body is greater. But if the limbs are moved while falling, the body is less damaged. So that if a body falling from a great height should be moved from the vertical trajectory of its descent by some force acting on it, it suffers less harm, and this is shown by experience.

This is only an excerpt from a long disquisition on the miracle, and this miracle was only one of many discussed. It demonstrates very well the abstract, analytical, and objective style of developed scholastic thinking. The fourteenth century saw much original speculation in the field of dynamics and this snippet from the musings of a papal official at Avignon shows how widely this style of thought had spread among educated clerics of the time.

The debates over falling bodies, the lists of relevant documents, the letters of persuasion from kings and bishops, the careful consideration of cardinals—all this eventually came to an end in 1320, when a decision was made. Thomas de Cantilupe was a saint. John XXII (1316–34), successor to Pope Clement V, who had initiated the canonization process, was finally convinced. The account of this last lap tells how the pope and cardinals went through the evidence about Cantilupe's life and miracles, how they agreed that it was soundly based, how Pope John then consulted with the cardinals who were absent from Avignon, and finally how the Lord John, in consistory at Avignon, after having consulted the absent cardinals, came down from his seat, put aside his mitre, and knelt, while all the cardinals knelt in their places, and pronounced as follows: "To the honor of the Holy Trinity and the blessed Mary and the blessed apostles Peter and Paul and of all saints and in exaltation of the faith, we declare by apostolic authority that so many and so great things have been proven about the life and miracles of Saint Thomas de Cantilupe, bishop of Hereford, that they suffice for his canonization. We declare by the same authority that we should proceed to his canonization."

On 17 April 1320 Pope John went to the main church of Avignon and there formally canonized Thomas de Cantilupe. The same day he celebrated the mass of the new saint for the first time and issued the bull announcing the canonization.

Aftermath

Many of the players in the story of the hanged man's miraculous resurrection had died before the canonization inquest of 1307 took place. They appear in the evidence as "those who had died earlier" (*praemortui*); that is, between the events of 1290 and the hearings of 1307. Some were centrally important, such as William de Briouze senior, the catalyst of the action and dead for more than sixteen years when the commissioners began their work. Others, like the deceased ladies-in-waiting of Lady Mary or the armed men in John de Baggeham's detachment at the foot of the gallows, had small but significant minor roles. Their stories could not now be told except through the words of those who did survive until 1307. The most prominent of "those who had died earlier" was, of course, Trahaearn ap Hywel, the Welsh nobleman and rebel whose kindred had not managed to save him from the ignominy of hanging. He is the shadow of William Cragh. Cragh's story was remarkable but he lived on only in poverty and oppression. Trahaearn died on the gallows and never strutted on the stage that the papal commission offered, but his death and his noble status were recalled for many years and he did not fade away into the destitution of William Cragh.

Of those who actually participated in the hearings on this case during the canonization process, we can distinguish the following groups:

THE COMMISSIONERS: William Durand, bishop of Mende; Ralph Baldock, bishop of London; William de Testa, archdeacon of Aran;

THE NOTARIES: William le Dorturer of Selborne; Adam of Lindsey; Raymond de la Prada; Ranulf Daniel of Waltham Holy Cross;

OTHER MEMBERS OF THE COMMISSION: Raymond Barroti, precentor of Mende; Raymond Berengar, monk of Figeac, chaplain of William Durand; William de Melford, chancellor of the bishop of London; Gilbert de Brueria, beneficed priest;

THE INTERPRETERS: English friars; John Young or (in Welsh) Sion Ieuanc and Maurice of Pencoyd, Welsh friars from Hereford;

THE HEREFORD CLERGY: notably Henry of Schorne, proctor in the case;

THE WITNESSES: at London Lady Mary de Briouze, dowager of Bramber and Gower; William de Briouze junior, lord of Bramber and Gower; William of Codineston, rector of Findon; at Hereford William Cragh, the hanged man; Thomas Marshall, poor priest of Swansea; John of Baggeham, steward of the de Briouze household in Gower; Henry Skinner, a propertied man of Swansea; Adam of Loughor, a craftsman of Swansea; John ap Hywel, a hired laborer of Swansea.

The canonization inquiry had thus temporarily brought together two prominent ecclesiastics from the south of France, a Marcher baron and his stepmother, a well-off Sussex clergyman, notaries from England and France, some propertied inhabitants of Swansea, a poor priest, a laborer, from southern Wales, a mono-glot Welsh rebel, some Welsh friars, and the bishop of London and his clerks. After 1307 they went their separate ways. Many returned to the local worlds from which they had briefly emerged into the light of scrutiny during the canonization process, while others, the more powerful and wealthy, can be traced in the fol-lowing years.

The later tales of these major figures are constantly interwoven with the great political incidents of the time: the removal of the papacy to Avignon in 1309, the general council held at Vienne from 1311–1312, the suppression of the Templars—the first of the crusading orders to be done away with as it was the first to be formed—, the wars of the English and the Scots, the civil strife under Edward II of England. On occasion the paths of the three commissioners crossed again, although their destinies were to be rather different, and three different and widely separated countries were to house their tombs.

William Durand

William Durand continued to be employed by the papacy for important commissions. His first major task after the canonization process of Thomas de Cantilupe was the inquiry into the Order of Knights Templar. The Templars had been founded around 1120, in the early days of the crusading movement, to protect pilgrims to Jerusalem from Muslim attack, and had gradually become an immensely wealthy and politically powerful organization. The Order provided the backbone of the military forces of the crusader states down to their final conquest, and served as bankers to kings. The Rue du Temple in Paris and the Inner Temple and Middle Temple in London are mementos of two of the most important of the Order's houses.

The annihilation of the crusader states in Palestine and Syria by the Mamluks of Egypt in 1291 (the year after William Cragh's miraculous revival) predictably caused a crisis in the crusading movement and prompted self-doubt and questioning among Catholic Christians. They did not ask if crusading was right but rather, why it had failed. Among the most closely scrutinized crusading institutions were the crusading orders. Reflection turned to crisis when the dominant ruler in western Europe, Philip IV of France, decided, either from avarice or fanaticism, that the Templars were devilish deviants who had to be broken. In October 1307, while the canonization commissioners were dutifully questioning the witnesses in Hereford, all the Templars in France were rounded up and accused of blasphemy, idolatry, and sodomy. Under torture some of them confessed.

In November 1307, after a period of prevarication, Clement V decided to attempt to take the matter into his own hands. He commanded the rulers of Christendom to arrest all Templars and sequester their property, since he had heard many allegations against them. The following August, after months of negotiation and deliberation, he instituted his own inquest into the Order, commissioning eight important ecclesiastics to undertake it. Among them was William Durand, bishop of Mende. Returned to France, the bishop now continued his assiduous and varied service to the first of the Avignon popes. The inquest was long and complex, beginning its hearings only a year after it was appointed and continuing for almost two (August 1309 through June 1311). Although it was investigating blasphemy rather than sanctity, it had many formal features in common with the inquiry into Thomas de Cantilupe, including some of the same standard questions.

While the questionnaire used in the Cantilupe process had twenty-five questions (articles), in the case of the Templars 127 articles were reviewed: did Templars spit on the crucifix? Did they urinate on the crucifix? Did they worship a cat? When a new brother was received into the Order did he kiss the brother who received him on the mouth? Or the belly? Or the anus? Or the penis? Not all the questions were so sensational, but they reveal they same obsessive pursuit of detail that animated the commissioners when they tried to find out whether William Cragh's body was carried from the gallows on a wheel, a ladder, or in some other way. The inquisitorial machine *was* a machine and if it caught hold of your sleeve, it would end up dragging in your whole body.

The articles were read to the Templars under examination first in Latin, then in French—the linguistic situation was less complex than that in England and Wales, where the universal language of authority, Latin, coexisted with both a high status learned language (French) and various vernaculars (English, Welsh). There were many witnesses to be heard, 127 articles to be investigated, and occasional breaks and recesses to be taken. Philip IV was unwilling to await the outcome of such a slow and judicious process; in May 1310, in the middle of the papal inquiry, sixty Templars were burned in Paris at the indirect but unmistakable behest of the king. This action was legal, for the pope had authorized local bishops to act against individual Templars while the commission investigated the Order as a whole, and it was the archbishop of Sens who was technically responsible for the executions.

The burning flesh of their brothers left a permanent reek of fear among the surviving Templars, and the papal commissioners suddenly found few to give evidence in defence of the Order. Sometimes witnesses inexplicably retracted their evidence and confessed to the bizarre offences of which they were accused. They were in the hands of royal jailers between their bouts of interrogation by the commissioners and seem often to have been treated roughly. Although the papal commission continued its work, it served less and less as a genuine inquiry and increasingly as a court of record for frightened and demoralized defectors. By the time it concluded in the summer of 1311, the papal commission into the Order of the Templars had heard a total of 231 witnesses, just a few more than the 205 heard in the Cantilupe canonization process. Its results, just like those of the canonization inquiry of 1307, were written up by notaries. Two copies were made, a parchment roll that was sent off to the pope and a stout paper volume that was preserved in the treasury of the cathedral of Notre-Dame de Paris and is now to be found in the Bibliothèque nationale. The probing bureaucratic operations of the late medieval Church have left many such eloquent surviving witnesses.

In the same month that he authorized the papal commission of inquiry into the Templars, August 1308, Clement V issued a bull summoning the Council of Vienne, which was the only general council of the Catholic Church held in the 140 years between 1274 and 1414. A Catholic general council was an assembly of the chief ecclesiastics—archbishops, bishops, and important abbots—summoned by the pope to discuss matters of common concern, to make rulings on important issues, and often to establish an agreed policy on political problems confronting the Church. At Vienne the chief items on the agenda were heresy, crusade, and, naturally, the affair of the Templars. Its meetings lasted from October 1311 to May 1312 and from it emerged some fundamental documents on the life of the Church.

When he issued the summons to the Council of Vienne, Pope Clement also invited the bishops to communicate to him "all the things that seem useful to them for the good state of the Church and the Christian people and the exaltation of the faith." William Durand took the request seriously. His treatise *How to Conduct a General Council* is a wide-ranging review of the failings of the Church. It might seem surprising that this apparently establishment figure, who had been trained in the law, appointed to succeed his uncle as bishop, and entrusted with several important papal commissions, should produce a manifesto advocating that "above all else the things in the Church of God that need correction and reform should be corrected and reformed, both in head and limbs." The discrepancy is, however, only superficial. There were limits to William Durand's ideal of reform. He did not, in fact, think a radical revision of Catholic Christianity was required, but believed in something more limited and more in his own interests.

He was against the centralized power of the papacy and suggested that, as a way of limiting papal monarchy, a general council be held every ten years. Subsequent reformers looked back on this proposal as a trailblazing call to amend the constitution of the Church. Nearer the time, his true impulses were more evident. Pope Clement's successor, John XXII, described Durand's recommendations as an attempt to create a "schism between pope and bishops" and referred to "the book he had fabricated against the pope and the Holy See." Ever since the middle of the eleventh century, the time of the so-called papal reform, the power of the pope had increased at the expense of the power of the bishops. William Durand was unhappy with this situation. He declared that the bishops had inherited the authority given to the apostles by Jesus and that the other apostles had received just as much power as Peter, who had given power to popes. William Durand's reservations about papal power were genuine. Some of his other proposals for reform, however, have a more hypocritical flavor. He argues, for instance, that no church office should be granted to one who could not speak the local language, but official records reveal that he secured the Irish archdeaconry of

Armagh for his cousin William Carrerie, who presumably spoke only French and Latin.

Whatever the long-term influence of William Durand's treatise on reform, the course of events at the Council of Vienne was shaped not by the considered recommendations of the attendant clergy but by the looming presence of the king of France, Philip IV, who summoned the French States-General (the equivalent of the English parliament) to Lyons, a mere sixteen miles from Vienne. While the Council was sitting, he made visits to Vienne and had secret meetings with the pope, the records of which were subsequently destroyed. The outcome is clear. On 22 March 1312 Clement V issued a bull (*Vox in excelso*) completely suppressing the Templars—"the Order, its rule, its habit, and its name." Soon thereafter its properties were transferred to the Hospitallers, the other major crusading order. Even this did not halt Philip IV's obsessional pursuit. In the spring of 1314 Jacques de Molay, last grand master of the Templars, was burned alive in Paris. Within nine months, however, both the pope and the king of France were dead. The victim, the tyrant, and the unsteady pontiff had all left the scene.

William Durand, however, continued. He was employed by subsequent kings of France in negotiations with neighboring powers and, though his relations with John XXII, elected pope in 1316, were never as close as those he had enjoyed with Clement V, he served as an effective link between the new kings of France and the new, if aged, pope. In 1320 he returned to England in connection with the final stage of the canonization of Thomas de Cantilupe. The following year he was back again, "to make peace between the king of England and Lord Robert Bruce." Another problem which occupied him was the crusade. His treatise on general councils shows his taste for paper plans and another policy paper of this type is William's memorandum on how to conduct a crusade. He envisages a great new crusade headed by, and largely funded by, the king of France. Before the expedition begins, he suggests, peace is to be established among all Christian rulers "by the Roman Church and by the illustrious lord king of

France." Kings who might pose a threat to "this kingdom" (France) are to be encouraged to go ahead on crusade. The French king is not only to provide financial help for the prelates and nobles of France for the expedition but also to make provision for "those who are not of this kingdom."

Some of Durand's crusading recommendations are simple and practical military suggestions: there should be a good stock of ships and war machines, and an embargo should be placed on trade with Muslim countries. Others concern the moral purification necessary for holy war: austere clothing, good money, sensible dowries, prudent administration—all these will make the crusaders better prepared and more likely to succeed. Lastly there are a large number of provisions concerning the importance of high ecclesiastics going on the crusade and suggestions for lightening their financial burdens when they did so.

William Durand was not only a theorist of the crusade. In the 1320s he was also given the task of organizing a real crusading expedition to the eastern Mediterranean. In 1329, as part of this endeavor, he set out for the kingdom of Cyprus, the only surviving crusader state, protected from Mamluk power by its island situation. He went with a large entourage in a group of Genoese galleys that were also conveying a bride to the heir of the kingdom. He never returned. After participating in a mysterious embassy to the sultan of Egypt, he died in Cyprus in 1330 and was buried in the church of the Cistercians in Nicosia. His epitaph could be read there as late as the seventeenth century.

Bishop of his southern French diocese for over thirty years, William Durand had been an emissary and representative of both pope and king of France, and an active agent in the suppression of the Templars, in the negotiations between England and Scotland, and in the snarled attempts to launch a new crusading expedition. Buried far from home twenty-three years after the canonization hearings, he had perhaps rarely thought of the case of William Cragh in the intervening years or played over in his mind the curious sing-song of the Welsh he had heard in Hereford so long before. He had been a busy man.

Ralph Baldock

Like William Durand, Ralph Baldock was involved in the trial and dissolution of the Order of the Templars. The newly crowned English king, Edward II, was initially skeptical of the "abominable and hateful things said" against the Templars but, after receipt of a papal bull authorizing their arrest, he complied. All Templars were to be taken into custody on 10 January 1308.[10] The only Templar property in Gower was Llanmadoc, not far from William Cragh's parish of Llanrhidian, which had been granted to the Order by the dowager countess of Warwick in 1156, at the time when the earls of Warwick possessed Gower. Now, in accordance with royal instructions, the sheriff of Carmarthen rode over to Llanmadoc with a posse of twelve men and seized the manor into the king's hands (eventually it came into the possession of the Hospitallers, with whom it remained until the Reformation).

Despite the brisk seizure of the Order's property and personnel, the campaign against the Templars in England proceeded very slowly. The two inquisitors assigned to investigate the charges against them, a French abbot and canon, arrived in England only on 13 September 1309, more than twenty months after the arrests. Several English bishops, including Ralph Baldock of London, joined them in their task. Once again he would be sitting alongside French ecclesiastics in a papally instigated inquiry.

Between October 1309 and June 1310 Bishop Baldock and the two inquisitors questioned forty-seven Templars, many of them repeatedly, at the Church of the Holy Trinity in Aldgate and elsewhere in London, but they encountered very little damning evidence. English trials did not allow the use of torture on suspects and this was a great obstacle to obtaining confessions, especially to the bizarre and elaborate charges framed against the Templars. Neither French nor papal courts had such an inhibition and throughout 1310 the two French inquisitors in the case, with the backing of the pope, pressed for torture to be permitted in their interrogation. The king made some concessions in this respect and eventually, in June 1311, some fugitive Templars provided the necessary confessions. They were interrogated before the bishops of London and Chichester, confessed, and recanted. The other Templars now followed suit. Bishop Ralph was not the only figure to be involved in both the canonization process of Cantilupe and the trial of the English Templars: the proceedings of 1309–10 were recorded by the notary Adam of Lindsey and those of 1311 by Ranulf of Waltham, both of whom had been notaries for the process of 1307, while William le Dorturer, another notary in the Cantilupe case, and Gilbert de Brueria, a member of the commission, appeared as witnesses in the trial of the Templars.

While he was thus deeply involved in the case of the Templars, Ralph Baldock was also concerned, to some extent, with the political conflicts between Edward II and his baronial opponents. The new king had a taste for "favorites"—young courtiers on whom he showered favors and affection—the first being the notorious Piers Gaveston, whom the king's baronial opponents hated deeply. In March 1310 a widely based movement of opposition secured the king's unwilling consent to the appointment of a committee of bishops and barons "at whose judgment and command the state of the realm should be reformed and strengthened." In the following year this committee, the Ordainers, drew up proposals for reform, including the banishment of Gaveston. Ralph Baldock was one of the Ordainers but does not appear to have been an opponent of the king; although he had been replaced as royal chancellor after the new king's accession, in the midst of the Cantilupe canonization hearings, this does not seem to have indicated a particular personal antipathy. Moreover, the Ordainers included prelates and barons of a variety of views. Seven bishops were among them, and the bishop of London would perhaps be an odd exclusion.

Like William Durand, Bishop Ralph attended the great Council of Vienne in 1311. On 19 August 1311 he wrote from the episcopal manor of Stepney to the abbot and canons of Saint Osyth in Essex, requesting their prayers, "since we are now getting ready to set out on the journey to the general council." This letter to Saint Osyth's is of especial interest to those following the case of Thomas de Cantilupe, for its main purpose is to make arrangements about the boy Roger of Conway, "whom God, through the merits of Thomas de Cantilupe, . . . revived from the dead." Bishop Ralph asked the abbot of Saint Osyth to provide an annual sum of £4 to support the boy, payable to Thomas of Leighton, "a minor canon in our church of London, to whom we have entrusted Roger to be educated and instructed in letters and manners." The plan was that eventually Roger of Conway would receive an ecclesiastical benefice. Saint Thomas had saved the boy's life and the bishop-commissioner wished to make sure it was a comfortable one.

The case of Roger of Conway is fully reported in the record of the canonization proceedings. As a toddler aged two years and three months, he had fallen into the moat of Edward I's castle at Conway, which the king had built in the 1280s in the aftermath of his conquest of Wales. Thanks to the intervention of Thomas de Cantilupe, the child had been revived. This accident had taken place on 6 September 1303, so Roger would be six years old when he came before the bishop of London and the other commissioners in Hereford in 1307. Obviously some arrangement had been made with Roger's parents, so that the boy was entrusted to the care of the bishop. In the summer of 1311, when Bishop Baldock was preparing for his trip to Vienne and securing financial support from Saint Osyth's, Roger would be a boy of ten. His is a curious fortune: born to an English family in service in one of Edward I's new conquest castles (his father was the cook to the constable of the castle), adopted by a bishop of London, and brought up for a clerical career among the canons of Saint Paul's.

Bishop Baldock's register survives to this day and shows the many everyday issues that would occupy a busy bishop. The trial of the Templars, the friction between Edward II and his opponents, and the general council of Vienne were great public events, but the pages of the register also show the bishop dealing with criminal charges against the local clergy, supervising the monasteries of his diocese, and protecting his own rights. He had to ban the "wrestling matches, dancing, and jesting" which were taking place in Barking churchyard (he had heard about them through the "public reputation" or *fama* of the type discussed in chapter 10), while royal records reveal a vigorous dispute over the bishop's ancient right to keep the flesh of whales washed up on his lands when one unfortunate creature was stranded at Stepney in the summer of 1309. Along with all this, Ralph Baldock continued to be active as a tax collector, channeling the clerical income tax to the king and the pope, in the latter case through the hands of his former fellow commissioner William de Testa.

Bishop Baldock died at his manor house in Stepney on 24 July 1313. The bequest he made to his cathedral of 126 scholarly books shows the range of his intellectual interests. They included bibles, bible commentaries, theology tomes, saints' lives, books of canon and Roman law, sermons, and works on astronomy, medicine, and the natural world. An interest in English history is indicated by "Bede in English" and a copy of the chronicle of the twelfth-century historian Henry of Huntingdon. The books contained in his study at the time of his death—sermons, his register, records of the taxation of the diocese of London and the estates of the see, as well as of the trial of the Templars—reflect his professional activities. The precious ornaments he kept there also bring us back to the canonization process in which he had participated six years earlier, for they include "a portable altar made of jasper and containing precious relics; this used to belong to Thomas de Cantilupe, of good memory."

William de Testa

William de Testa continued to be active as the chief papal tax collector in the British Isles both during and after his service on the canonization inquiry. Some of his accounts survive, and papal letters acknowledge thousands of florins being received at the papal court in the south of France (the florin was an acceptably international currency into which English pennies were changed). Testing the sanctity of Thomas de Cantilupe and funding the papacy occurred simultaneously. In August 1307, for instance, at the height of the hearings, the pope commanded William and his colleagues to commandeer the goods of the Riccardi, an Italian trading company that had collapsed still owing debts to the papacy. Since William used the house of the dean of Saint Paul's as his base, having a strongroom specially constructed there, he would maintain regular contact with Bishop Ralph Baldock.

In return for this steadfast service he received numerous grants and privileges. Some were intended to help him in his work, such as the permission he received from the pope to have four clerks in his household who could draw their income from their ecclesiastical benefices but needed not be resident. Others were more personal, such as the right to his own private confessor. Most important were lucrative ecclesiastical offices. The position of precentor in Lincoln Cathedral and the archdeaconry of Ely were added to his archdeaconry of Aran, and he drew their revenues for the rest of his life, even after returning to France. His relatives benefited too, with his nephew Vitalis de Testa picking up several wealthy churches and becoming dean of London (although in the face of some opposition).

William de Testa's hard work as a papal tax collector finally won him a great reward. On 23 December 1312 Clement V created a number of cardinals, including among them William, who was promoted to cardinal-priest of Saint Cyriacus. In a letter of the following year the pope explicitly recognized that this elevation was on account of the industry and loyalty he had shown in his years in England. Finally relinquishing his position as tax collector for the British Isles in March 1313, after seven years' service, the new cardinal returned to the south of France and took up his position in the consistory of Clement V—the first Avignon pope, and one followed by a long line of southern French incumbents. Clement died in 1314 and the Gascon cardinals he had appointed, such as William de Testa, were never in great favor with his successor, John XXII, but William persevered in his duties, being an acknoweldged expert on relations between the pope and the English court. The experience he had acquired in the canonization process of Thomas de Cantilupe was tapped again in 1318, when he was one of the three cardinals entrusted with the task of examining the preliminary dossier prior to the canonization process of Thomas Aquinas (which eventually resulted in Aquinas's canonization in 1323).

On 1 September 1326 William de Testa drew up his will in his house at Avignon. The bequests he made show something of his priorities. First came the hospital of Saint James, which he had founded in his native city of Condom. This is where William wished to be buried, "in a tomb that is not too expensive nor too cheap and whose appearance, along with his epitaph, will prompt people to pray for him more devoutly." A huge range of churches and religious communities in Condom, Comminges, and Avignon benefited from his bequests. His nephews were not forgotten, especially Paul, who received the cardinal's best horse and was expected to take charge of the hospital at Condom. The English connection crops up in a few provisions, such as the bequest to his proctor in England and the grant for repairing William's houses and churches at Spofforth in Yorkshire, "which had been destroyed by the Scots and other wicked men." He commended his soul to God, the Virgin Mary, Saints Peter and Paul, Saint James (the patron of his hospital), Saint Mary Magdalene (associated in legend with Provence), Saint Bertrand (patron of the diocese of Comminges, where William held the archdeaconry of Aran), Saint Cyriacus (the patron of his cardinal church), and Saint Quiteria (an obscure but definitely Gascon virgin martyr). He thus placed himself confidently in the hands of both the chief saints and the local saints.

William de Testa is a good example of the ecclesiastics who made the fourteenth-century Church what it was. He moved from the local hierarchy of the diocese of Comminges onto the international scene through the patronage of his fellow Gascon, the bishop of Comminges who became Pope Clement V. William de Testa served assiduously in the British Isles, squeezing money from the clergy and remitting most of it to the king and the substantial remainder to his papal patron. In return he accumulated many lucrative ecclesiastical offices for himself and his nephews. One consequence was that the archdeaconry of Ely in the English Fenland was held by this southern French prelate for thirteen years when he was resident not in Ely but in Avignon.

Acquiring the high office of cardinal, William gave generously to his home town, represented sectional interests at the papal court, and performed his official tasks. Bureaucrat, official, administrator, patron of his relatives and his birthplace, he was also instrumental in promoting both Thomas de Cantilupe and Thomas Aquinas to sainthood.

William and Mary de Briouze

In the years immediately following 1307, the year in which they gave their evidence in the chapter-house of Saint Paul's in London, William and Mary de Briouze seem to have lived lives that were in no way exceptional for their class. William continued to provide support for the apparently endless war against the Scots, while he and his stepmother engaged in the equally interminable litigation between relatives that consumed much of the time and energy of English landholders. Especially prolonged lawsuits resulted from the claims of Mary's son Peter and of his heir, Thomas (Thomas was still pursuing one of these disputes in the late 1330s).

After granting the charters of 1306 to his tenants in Gower (as discussed in chapter 8), William de Briouze appears to have enjoyed better relations within his Welsh lordship. Several documents that he issued at this time show him in Gower at Oystermouth, which he developed as an important residence, probably building the elegant chapel block there. By 1315 he would be in his mid-fifties and the main question preoccupying him would be the succession to his estates. There is evidence that William had a son, also called William. He was old enough to be summoned to the campaign against the Scots in 1311 but since there is no trace of him after 1315 and since in the year 1316 William made complex arrangements to transmit his property after his death to one of his daughters, the implication is that William the son died in late 1315 or early 1316, leaving William the father with no male heirs.

The decisions that William de Briouze made about the transmission of his lands in the years 1316–20 eventually led to one of the major political crises of Edward II's reign. William's own motives in this were personal rather than political. On the one hand, he wished to ensure the succession of his daughter Alina and her husband, the young Baron John de Mowbray, lord of Axholme in Lincolnshire, Thirsk in Yorkshire, Melton Mowbray in Leicestershire, and many other manors besides. John was obviously eager to add Bramber and Gower to his estates and a series of documents was drawn up to ensure that this would happen smoothly when William de Briouze died. On the other hand, William wanted to provide for himself during his lifetime. He needed the security of some lands for life and a supply of cash.

It is this last requirement—a supply of cash—that seems to have created the complications. William de Briouze had a reputation as a poor manager of money—"very rich by descent but a dissipater of the property left to him," as one chronicler puts it—and the records bear this out. Among William's earliest appearances in written sources, in the mid-1280s, are his acknowledgments of various debts, including one to a Florentine merchant, and forty years later, in 1323, an interesting correspondence preserved in the archives of Canterbury Cathedral reveals him selling off the manor of Wickhambreux to the highest bidder. It appears that he wished to make as much profit as he could from the disposal of the lordship of Gower. He granted it by charter to John de Mowbray and Alina but also sold the reversion of the estate to the earl of Hereford if they died without issue. Contemporaries even talk of his "offering it for sale to many lords."

The situation would have been less explosive if Gower had not become one of the objectives of Edward II's latest favorite, Hugh Despenser the Younger. Edward's best known favorite, Piers Gaveston, had been killed in 1312 by baronial opponents of the king who resented his intimacy with the monarch and his rapid rise to power and wealth, but in the following years the two Despensers, father and son, gradually came to dominate the king and enjoy his favor in a way just as exasperating to the baronial opposition. Hugh Despenser the Younger was a contemporary of Edward's and had been in his household when he was Prince of Wales. He had been given as a bride the sister of the earl of

Gloucester and when the earl was killed at Bannockburn in 1314, Hugh Despenser made it his goal to secure the Gloucester heritage, including the vast southern Welsh lands. Gower would round off his holdings neatly.

An aging, impecunious, and irresponsible baron, a young and impatient son-in-law, and a high-handed and ruthless royal favorite made the competition for Gower a combustible issue. In the autumn of 1320 John de Mowbray entered into possession of Gower. In response the king, at Despenser's instigation, seized the lordship, saying that it was not lawful for barons to alienate their lands without royal consent. The Marcher lords were outraged, disputed this reading of the law, and, in the spring of 1321, went into open rebellion. Despenser's lordship of Glamorgan was conquered, John de Mowbray seized Gower back and by the summer Edward had to submit to the opposition and exile the Despensers.

The king's defeat was only temporary. In the last months of 1321 he began to rebuild his military power and in December, recalled the Despensers. His opponents lacked coordination and the most powerful of them, the king's obstructive but indecisive cousin, Thomas of Lancaster, did not give adequate leadership. Gower was reoccupied by royal troops in February 1322 and the following month, on 16 March, the rebels were decisively defeated at Boroughbridge in Yorkshire. In the aftermath Thomas of Lancaster was beheaded but many of the other baronial and knightly captives were hanged, among them John de Mowbray, who was dragged through the streets of York and suspended in iron chains until his body rotted. Hanging was a shameful form of execution, not fit for a gentleman. William de Briouze junior had been glad enough to see his father hang William Cragh and the Welsh noble Trahaearn ap Hywel in 1290; it is unlikely that he imagined his own son-in-law would face the same death in 1322.

The four years 1322–26 saw a royalist reaction and the triumph of the Despensers. The elder Hugh was created earl of Winchester, while both father and son were enriched with the lands of the rebels and of anyone else who came within their range. By a series of legal transactions too convoluted to describe in detail, they fastened their claws on practically the whole de Briouze estate, including the manors that William de Briouze held for life and those that Lady Mary had as dower. John de Mowbray's widow, Alina, was kept in prison with her young son, also John, until she conceded her rights to the Despensers. Thus when William de Briouze died, aged about sixty-five, in the spring of 1326, the barony of Bramber was described as "of the inheritance of Hugh Despenser, earl of Winchester." Lady Mary died just a few weeks after her stepson. In fact, the surveys of their estates undertaken at their deaths by order of the royal government now nestle beside each other in the Public Record Office, achieving a closer proximity than the two protagonists seem to have desired in life. Lady Mary's lands, too, were described as part of the Despenser inheritance.

If William and Mary de Briouze had lived just six months longer, they would have witnessed a political revolution as great as that of 1322 and one that saw the restoration of Bramber and Gower to Alina and her son, John de Mowbray junior. Edward II's estranged queen, Isabella of France, landed in England on 24 September 1326 and within a few months the king's support faded away. In October Hugh Despenser the Elder was hanged at Bristol and the following month his son was strung up on an especially high gallows at Hereford, within sight of the cathedral that housed the remains of the new saint, Thomas de Cantilupe.

The canonization of Thomas de Cantilupe was a long process, which generated thousands of words—among them the words that form the basis of this book. In the winter of 1290 a Welsh rebel had been led out to be hanged on a hill outside Swansea. In 1307 a committee of literate, highly educated clergy questioned the surviving witnesses about this event. It was an incident like all historical moments: unique, and also an intersection of many paths. Looked at one way, it concerns the colonial subjection of the Welsh to the English; from another, the relationships within an irritable aristocratic family; and from yet another, the growth of a new saintly cult. We see the late medieval papacy at its most

bureaucratic and baroque, scholastic thinkers at their most re-
fined, the mechanics of execution at its most graphic. Men, and
one woman, from the richest to the poorest and from the most
cosmopolitan to the most local, had been squeezed together for
a moment. They were buried in Cyprus, in Condom, in London,
in Swansea. By 1330, when William Durand died, it is unlikely
that many survivors of the event of 1290 or the inquest of 1307
existed. All that remains now is the carefully preserved record of
the inquest, drowsing in the Vatican Library, an inquest inspired
by the urge to make the dead man, Thomas de Cantilupe, live as
a saint; it allows the voices of many dead men, from William de
Testa, tax collector and cardinal, to William Cragh, defeated
Welsh rebel, to speak again.

Notes

The main source on which this story is based is the record of the canonization process of Thomas de Cantilupe contained in MS Vatican City, Biblioteca Apostolica Vaticana, Vat. Lat. 4015. The relevant testimony is on fols. 7v–14v and 219v–227v, the latter partly printed in *Acta sanctorum, Octobris* 1, pp. 633–37. Only when the present work was well advanced did it become clear that this story was generating a small cottage industry among historians. The tale of William Cragh is discussed by Professor Michael Richter of Constance in "Waliser und Wundermänner um 1300," in *Spannungen und Widersprüche: Gedenkschrift für Frantisek Graus*, ed. S. Burghartz et al. (Sigmaringen, 1992), pp. 23–36 (a reference kindly supplied by Professor John Gillingham), and the Latin text of the testimony has been printed by Professor Richter in "William ap Rhys, William de Braose, and the Lordship of Gower, 1289 and 1307," *Studia Celtica* 32 (1998), 189–209 (his dating of 1289 differs from mine of 1290, argued here). Professor Michael Goodich of the University of Haifa has also analyzed the tale and was good enough to send his typescript. See also Jussi Hanska, "The Hanging of William Cragh: Anatomy of a Miracle," *Journal of Medieval History* 27 (2001): 121–38.

Work in Rome was funded by the University of Saint Andrews and a Caledonian Research Foundation Fellowship from the Royal Society of Edinburgh. Paul Brand, Chris Given-Wilson, and John Hudson provided much valued advice on a variety of topics.

The following abbreviations have been used:

BL	British Library
Brut	*Brut y Tywysogyon or The Chronicle of the Princes: Red Book of Hergest Version*, ed. Thomas Jones (Cardiff, 1955)
Cartae	*Cartae et alia munimenta quae ad dominium de Glamorgancia pertinent*, ed. G. T. Clark (6 vols., Cardiff, 1910)

PRO   Public Record Office, London
Rot. Parl.   *Rotuli Parliamentorum* (6 vols.)
RS   Rolls Series

Chapter 1. The Story

Page

1 In general on Thomas de Cantilupe and his cult see Ronald C. Finu-
cane, *Miracles and Pilgrims: Popular Beliefs in Medieval England*
(London and Totowa, 1977), pp. 173–88; Michael Richter, *Sprache
und Gesellschaft im Mittelalter* (Stuttgart, 1979), pp. 171–217; *St.
Thomas Cantilupe, Bishop of Hereford: Essays in His Honour*, ed.
Meryl Jancey (Hereford, 1982). For details on the cult in the late
Middle Ages, see R. N. Swanson, "Devotional Offerings at Here-
ford Cathedral in the Later Middle Ages," *Analecta Bollandiana*
III (1993): 93–102.

3 On William de Briouze and Llywelyn's wife see *Brut*, p. 229.

3–4 For the revolt of Rhys ap Maredudd see the discussion in
chapter 3.

9 Sunehild: *Sonehud* is the form in the testimony of Lady Mary, *Sonau-
tam* in that of her stepson. Peter McClure kindly provided expert
advice on this name.

Chapter 2. The Questioners

Page

14 Dossier on Gilbert of Sempringham: *Book of St Gilbert*, ed. Ray-
monde Foreville and Gillian Keir, Oxford Medieval Texts (1987).

14 "you may not revere anyone as a saint": *Decretales* 3. 45. 1, ed.
E. Friedberg, Corpus iuris canonici 2 (Leipzig, 1881), col. 650.

14 The standard account of medieval canonization processes is André
Vauchez, *Sainthood in the Late Middle Ages* (Eng. trans., Cambridge, 1997).

15 The papal letter of 23 August 1306 is Hereford Cathedral Archives
1441; work in the archives was greatly aided by the helpfulness of
the archivist, Rosalind Caird, and the librarian, Joan Williams.

15 On William of Gainsborough see *The Register of William de Geynes-
burgh, Bishop of Worcester, 1302–1307*, ed. J.W.W. Bund, Worces-
tershire Historical Society 19 (1907–29); the words cited are from
Vatican City, Biblioteca Apostolica Vaticana, MS Vat. Lat. 4016,
fol. 63v.

16 On the life of William Durand the Younger see P. Viollet, "Guillaume Durant le Jeune, évêque de Mende," *Histoire littéraire de la France* 35 (1921): 1–139; Constantine Fasolt, *Council and Hierarchy: The Political Thought of William Durant the Younger* (Cambridge, 1991), pp. 73–100.

17 Durand's settlement involving Camerino: *Vatikanische Aktenstücke zur italienischen Legation des Duranti und Pilifort d. J. 1305–1306*, ed. Ludwig Schnitte (Leobschütz, 1909), p. 30.

18 For references to Baldock's career see John Le Neve, *Fasti Ecclesiae Anglicanae, 1300–1541*, vol. 5, *St. Paul's, London*, compiled by Joyce M. Horn (London, 1963), p. 1; and for a fascinating sidelight, Richard W. Pfaff, "Bishop Baldock's Book, St Paul's Cathedral, and the Use of Sarum," in *Liturgical Calendars, Saints, and Services in Medieval England* (Aldershot, 1998), pp. 1–20 (no. 9).

18 The image at Ashingdon: *Registrum Radulphi Baldock, Gilberti Segrave, Ricardi Newport et Stephani Gravesend, episcoporum Londoniensium, 1304–1338*, ed. R. C. Fowler, Canterbury and York Soc. 7 (1911), pp. 25–26.

19 Baldock sworn onto king's council: *Rot. Parl.* 1: 219.

19 Baldock sealing writs as chancellor: *Calendar of the Patent Rolls 1301–1307*, pp. 518–19.

19 On the career of William de Testa see Adrien Clergeac, "Un cardinal condomois: Guillaume de Teste," *Revue de Gascogne* (1930): 145–58, 203–10; and, for his activities as a tax collector in England, W. E. Lunt, *Financial Relations of the Papacy with England*, 2 vols. (Cambridge, Mass., 1939–62), index s.v. "Testa."

20 William de Testa's mission of 1305: *Original Papal Letters in England, 1305–1415*, ed. P.N.R. Zutschi (Vatican City, 1990), no. 13.

Chapter 3. The Plot Thickens

Page

22 The date of William Durand's arrival in England: *Annales Londonienses*, ed. William Stubbs, *Chronicles of the Reigns of Edward I and Edward II*, 2 vols., RS (1882–83) 1:1–251, at p. 150.

23 The attack on William de Testa at the Carlisle Parliament: *Rot. Parl.* 1:220.

23 William de Testa's letter of 20 March 1307: Vatican City, Biblioteca Apostolica Vaticana, MS Vat. Lat. 4016, fol. 2v.

23 "to fleece the English churches": *Flores historiarum*, ed. H. R. Luard, 3 vols., RS (1890), 3:136.

24 Thomas de Cantilupe and the Jews: Vat. Lat. 4015, fols. 6v, 104v–105.

24–25 On Saint Katherine's Chapel see City of Hereford Archaeology Unit, *Hereford Cathedral: The Bishop's Cloister*, Hereford Archaeology Series 283 (June 1996).

25 Language usage in the canonization process is analyzed by Michael Richter, *Sprache und Gesellschaft im Mittelalter* (Stuttgart, 1979), pp. 171–217.

26 *Tinguiosus* is the Latin word used as a synonym for "Cragh"; Welsh *crach* is a plural or collective noun (singular *crachen*) meaning "scab(s)"; *tinguiosus* probably represents *tingniosus*, for *tineosus*, from *tinea*, "scab" (cf. French *teigne*); the advice of Richard Sharpe on this point is much valued.

31 John of Baggeham may derive his name from Baggeham in Knowlton, Dorset, a manor held by William de Briouze senior and his son Giles: *Calendar of Inquisitions Post Mortem* 4:214 (1305).

Chapter 4. An Autumn Day

Page

35 Compensation payments in Welsh law: *Welsh Medieval Law*, ed. A. W. Wade-Evans (Oxford, 1909), p. 192.

37 "a man may live many hours": *Thómas saga erkibyskups*, ed. Eirikr Magnússon, 2 vols., RS (1875–83), 2:115.

38 The Victorian textbook on the effects of hanging: A. S. Taylor, *The Principles and Practice of Medical Jurisprudence*, 4th ed. (London, 1894), pp. 34–36, 40, 44, as cited in V.A.C. Gatrell, *The Hanging Tree: Execution and the English People 1770–1868* (Oxford, 1994), p. 46.

Chapter 5. Death by Hanging

Page

42 For useful comparative material on hanging see, in particular, Henry Summerson, "Attitudes to Capital Punishment in England, 1200–1350," *Thirteenth Century England* 8 (2001), 123–33.

43 "one English writer of the thirteenth century": Thomas of Chobham, *Summa confessorum*, ed. F. Broomfield, Analecta mediaevalia Namurcensia 25 (Louvain, 1968), pp. 432–33.

43 Prisoners at the Châtelet in 1488–89: Esther Cohen, *Peaceable Domain, Certain Justice* (Hilversum, 1996), p. 91 n.8 ; cf eadem, *The Crossroads of Justice* (Leiden, 1993), p. 165.

43 Binding hands at the Châtelet: Rodrigue Lavoie, "Justice, criminalité et peine de mort en France au Moyen Age," in *Le sentiment de la mort au Moyen Age*, ed. Claude Sutto (Quebec, 1979), pp. 31–55, at p. 39.

44 Paris execution route: Esther Cohen, "Symbols of Culpability and the Universal Language of Justice: The Ritual of Public Executions in Late Medieval Europe," *History of European Ideas* 11 (1989): 407–16, at p. 410.

44 On the siting of German scaffolds, Richard Evans, *Rituals of Retribution: Capital Punishment in Germany, 1600–1987* (Oxford, 1996), pp. 77–78.

44 For Gallows Hills outside medieval Welsh towns: G. Melville Richards, "The Sites of Some Medieval Gallows," *Archaeologia Cambrensis* 113 (1964): 159–65.

44 "someone who is met on the way": Thomas of Chobham, *Summa confessorum*, ed. F. Broomfield, Analecta mediaevalia Namurcensia 25 (Louvain, 1968), pp. 432–33.

45 Newenham tenants: Henry Summerson, "Attitudes to Capital Punishment in England, 1200–1350," *Thirteenth Century England* 8 (2001): 127, citing BL Arundel 17, fol. 36v.

45 English manuscript of the eleventh century: BL Cotton Claudius B. iv, fol. 59, reproduced in *Medieval Panorama*, ed. Robert Bartlett (London, 2001), p. 106.

45 Saint Amand manuscript: Barbara Abou-El-Haj, *The Medieval Cult of Saints: Formations and Transformations*, (Cambridge, 1994), p. 400, fig. 157; the *Sachsenspiegel* scene is reproduced in *Medieval Panorama*, ed. Robert Bartlett, p. 252.

45 Worcester 1184: *Gesta regis Henrici secundi Benedicti abbatis*, ed. William Stubbs, 2 vols., RS (1867), 1:315.

45 Iron chain 1366: John of Reading, *Chronicon*, ed. James Tait, *Chronica Johannis de Reading et Anonymi Cantuariensis* (Manchester, 1914), pp. 175–76.

46 Wooden nooses: Bernard of Angers, *Liber miraculorum sancte Fidis* 1. 30, ed. Luca Robertini (Spoleto, 1994), p. 135.

46 The account of the hanging at Carmarthen is from John Laurence, *A History of Capital Punishment* (London, 1932), pp. 56–57.

46 The Italian jurists are Jacobus de Bellovisu and Lucas de Penna, cited in Dieter Marschall, *De laqueo rupto: Die mißlungene Hinrichtung durch den Strang*, Bonner Rechtswissenschaftliche Abhandlungen 79 (1968), pp. 37–41. A much earlier reference to immunity after

survival of hanging is in a capitualry of 808, *Monumenta Germaniae Historica*, Leges II/1/i, no. 52, n. 2, p. 139.

47 Reprieves of 1234 and 1363: *Close Rolls 1234–1237*, p. 6; Henry Knighton, *Chronicon*, ed. J. R. Lumby, 2 vols., RS (1889–95), 2: 119.

47 Executions at the Châtelet 1389–92: Rodrigue Lavoie, "Justice, criminalité et peine de mort en France au moyen âge," in *Le sentiment de la mort au moyen âge*, ed. Claude Sutto (Quebec, 1979), pp. 31–55, at pp. 38–39.

47 The execution of William de Marisco: Matthew Paris, *Chronica majora*, ed. Henry R. Luard, 7 vols., RS (1872–84), 4:196 (1242); cf. 3:498 (1238); Suzanne Lewis, *The Art of Matthew Paris in the "Chronica Majora"* (Berkeley, 1987), p. 235, fig. 151.

48 "not one but many deaths": Paris, *Chronica majora* 4, p. 197.

48 Execution of Dafydd ap Gruffudd: *Annals of Dunstable*, ed. H. R. Luard, *Annales monastici*, 3, RS (1866), p. 294.

48 Execution of William Wallace: *Annales Londonienses*, ed. William Stubbs, *Chronicles of the Reigns of Edward I and Edward II*, 2 vols., RS (1882–83) 1:141–42.

48–49 On the case of Cecco, *Acta sanctorum*, Aprilis 3, pp. 509–10.

49–50 "Analysis . . . of forty-two cases": Friedrich Lotter, "Heiliger und Gehenkter: Zur Todesstrafe in hagiographischen Episodenerzählungen des Mittelalters," in *Ecclesia et Regnum: Beiträge zur Geschichte von Kirche, Recht und Staat im Mittelalter. Festschrift für Franz-Josef Schmale*, ed. Dieter Berg and Hans-Werner Goetz (Bochum, 1989), pp. 1–19.

50–51 On Nicholas of Tolentino's miracles see Baudouin De Gaiffier, "Un thème hagiographique: le pendu miraculeusement sauvé," in *Etudes critiques d'hagiographie et d'iconologie* (Brussels, 1967), pp. 194–226, at pp. 218–20 and fig. 32.

51 Miracle of Saint Elizabeth of Thuringia: *Quellenstudien zur Geschichte der heiligen Elisabeth*, ed. Albert Huyskens (Marburg, 1908), pp. 255–57.

51 Resurrection in eleventh- and twelfth-century France: Pierre-André Sigal, *L'homme et le miracle dans la France médiévale: XIe.–XIIe. siècles* (Paris, 1985), pp. 253, 289.

52 Resurrection in canonization proceedings: André Vauchez, *Sainthood in the Late Middle Ages* (Eng. trans., Cambridge, 1997), p. 468, table 31.

Chapter 6. Time and Space

Page

55 "mimicking": Jacques Paul, "Expression et perception du temps d'après l'enquête sur les miracles de Louis d'Anjou," in *Temps, mémoire, tradition au Moyen Age* (Aix-en-Provence, 1983), pp. 19–41, at p. 23.

55 "be informed by another and follow him": *Henricus de Segusio Cardinalis Hostiensis in Secundum Decretalium librum commentaria* (Venice, 1581), fol. 105, cited by Christian Krötzl, "Kanonisationsprozess, Sozialgeschichte und Kanonisches Recht im Spätmittelalter," in *Nordic Perspectives on Medieval Canon Law*, ed. Mia Korpiola, Publications of Matthias Calonius Society 2 (Saarijärvi, 1999), pp. 19–39, at p. 22 n. 16.

55–57 The proof of age of Roger, son of Adam de Bavent, is in *Calendar of Inquisitions Post Mortem* 4: 35–37. Both Adam and Roger occur as witnesses to de Briouze charters: Oxford, Magdalene College, Sele Charters 53, 80; *Sir Christopher Hatton's Book of Seals*, ed. Lewis Loyd and Doris Stenton (Oxford, 1950), no. 315, pp. 217–18. Bavent is in the Calvados and Gunnor, the mother of William de Briouze, held land there in the time of William the Conqueror (*Regesta regum anglo-normannorum: The acta of William I (1066–1087)*, ed. David Bates [Oxford, 1998], no. 59, p. 281), so the link between the two families goes back to the eleventh century.

55–57 For further discussion of the memory tags in Proofs of Age see John Bedell, "Memory and Proof of Age in England 1272–1327," *Past and Present* 162 (1999): 3–27. For a contrasting situation, in which *anno Domini* dating was employed, see Jean-Marc Roger, "L'enquête sur l'âge de Jean II d'Estouteville (21–22 août 1397)," *Bulletin philologique et historique* (1975): 103–28 (a reference kindly supplied by Gadi Algazi).

57–58 The chronologically arranged record from Hereford is Oxford, Exeter College MS 158; this originally covered 1287–1305 (fols. 1–41) and this section was copied into the record of the 1307 process: Vat. Lat. 4015, fols. 265–308v. The Hereford collection was subsequently extended to 1309 (fols. 41–44) and 1312 (fols. 45–47v). The manuscript also contains the *relatio processus* (fols. 48v–59v), incomplete, and a stray miracle dating to 1404 (fol. 60).

57–58 The account of William Cragh's miracle is Oxford, Exeter College MS 158, fols. 18v–19; Vat. Lat. 4015, fols. 284–284v; *Acta sanctorum*, Octobris I, p. 676. The Exeter College manuscript has running heads for the year, commencing when the miracles began in April 1287 ("I annus," "II annus," etc.); the passage cited is in "IIII annus," that is, April 1290–April 1291, and can thus be securely dated to November and December 1290.

60 The death of William de Briouze at Findon at Epiphany 1291 is recorded in the Continuation of Gervase of Canterbury's *Gesta Regum*, ed. William Stubbs, *The Historical Works of Gervase of Canterbury*, 2 vols., RS (1879–80) 2:297.

60–61 On the transmission of the de Briouze estates in 1291: *Calendar of the Close Rolls 1288–1296*, pp. 157, 163, 196.

62 For the Rheims survey of 1422 see Pierre Desportes, "La population de Reims au XVe. siècle d'après un dénombrement de 1422," *Le Moyen Age* 72 (1966): 463–509.

64 "One German mile" in the miracles of Saint Elizabeth of Thuringia: *Quellenstudien zur Geschichte der heiligen Elisabeth*, ed. Albert Huyskens (Marburg, 1908), p. 255; the misunderstanding of time as space occurs as early as the *Legenda Aurea* of Jacobus de Voragine: c. 164 (aliter 158 and 168), ed. G. P. Maggioni, 2nd ed. (Florence, 1998), p. 1175.

Chapter 7. Colonial Wales

Page

64 For the history of the medieval lordship of Gower see *Glamorgan County History 3: The Middle Ages*, ed. T. B. Pugh (Cardiff, 1971), pp. 205–65. The map here is adapted from the one at the end of that volume.

69–70 Map of place-names: *Swansea and its Region*, ed. W.G.V. Balchin (Swansea, 1971), p. 152, fig. 25; comments on individual names in B. G. Charles, *Non-Celtic Place-Names in Wales* (London, 1938), pp. 114–31.

70 The grant of Llanrhidian by William de Turberville is mentioned in a confirmation charter by bishop Peter of Saint Davids (1176–98): *St. Davids Episcopal Acta 1085–1280*, ed. Julia Barrow (Cardiff, 1998), no. 46, p. 71. *Red Book of the Exchequer*, ed. Hubert Hall, 3 vols., RS (1896) 1:326, lists William de Turberville as a knight of the earl of Warwick after Henry of Gower and Henry du Neubourg, two landholders in Gower.

71 Attack by Gruffudd ap Rhys in 1116: *Brut*, p. 87.

71 For the Welsh attack on Gower in 1136 see *Gesta Stephani*, ed. K. R. Potter and R.H.C. Davis (Oxford, 1976), pp. 14–16.

71 Reconquest of Gower in the reign of King Stephen is mentioned in PRO E164/1, fol. 237v.

72 Rhys Ieuanc's attack of 1215: *Brut*, pp. 203–5.

73 Rhys Gryg's expulsion of the English: *Brut*, pp. 217–19.

74 John de Briouze's death: *Brut*, p. 231.

74 Llywelyn's attack on Gower of 1257 is described in *Annales Cambriae*, ed. J. W. ap Ithel, RS (1860), pp. 92–93.

74 *Annales Cambriae*, p. 95, for two hundred settlers killed.

74 For Llywelyn's career see J. Beverley Smith, *Llywelyn ap Gruffudd: Prince of Wales* (Cardiff, 1998).

74 *Calendar of the Patent Rolls 1272–1281*, p. 190, for William de Briouze on campaign in Wales in 1277.

74–75 *Calendar of the Patent Rolls 1281–1292*, p. 13, for William de Briouze's pilgrimage to Santiage; PRO C 47/2/4 , mm. 3–5, for troops from Gower in 1282.

75 Report on the rising of Rhys ap Maredudd by a chronicler from southern Wales in "Chronicle of the Thirteenth Century," *Archaeologia Cambrensis* 3rd ser. 8 (1862), pp. 272–83, at p. 281; for the rising in general see John E. Morris, "The Peace Settlement and Rhys's Rising," in *The Welsh Wars of Edward I* (Oxford, 1901), pp. 198–219; J. Beverley Smith, "The Origins of the Revolt of Rhys ap Maredudd," *Bulletin of the Board of Celtic Studies* 21 (1964–66): 151–63; Ralph A. Griffiths, "The Revolt of Rhys ap Maredudd, 1287–1288," *Welsh History Review* 3/ii (1966): 121–43 (repr. in his *Conquerors and Conquered in Medieval Wales* (1994), pp. 67–83).

76 "helm of Dinefwr": *Penguin Book of Welsh Verse*, trans. Anthony Conran (1967) p. 126 (Y Prydydd Bychan, Elegy for Rhys Gryg).

76 For the agreement of 1277, see *Littere Wallie*, ed. John Goronwy Edwards (Cardiff, 1940), no. 54, pp. 36–37.

76 *Annales Cambriae*, p. 107, on Rhys and war of 1282–83.

76 Rhys's renunciation of Dinefwr is in *Littere Wallie*, ed. John Goronwy Edwards (Cardiff, 1940), no. 212, p. 122.

77 Rhys' complaints to the king are printed in J. Beverley Smith, "The Origins of the Revolt of Rhys ap Maredudd," *Bulletin of the Board of Celtic Studies* 21 (1964–66): 151–63, at pp. 162–63.

77 The phrase "a manifest rebel and enemy of the king": *Calendar of Various Chancery Rolls: Supplementary Close Rolls, Welsh Rolls, Scutage Rolls 1277–1326* (London, 1912), p. 307.

77–78 Description of Rhys's raid on Gower in June 1287 from PRO E164/1, fol. 238.

78 The price of £100 that Edward I placed on Rhys's head: *Calendar of Various Chancery Rolls: Supplementary Close Rolls, Welsh Rolls, Scutage Rolls 1277–1326* (London, 1912), p. 307.

78 Letter of February 1289 regarding Rhys in Gower: ibid., p. 323.

79 The details of Rhys's trial in *Calendar of the Close Rolls 1288–96*, p. 267; the reward for his captors *Calendar of the Patent Rolls 1307–13*, p. 224; *Calendar of Inquisitions Post Mortem* 2: 21. *Brut y Tywysogyon or The Chronicle of the Princes: Peniarth MS 20 Version*, ed. Thomas Jones (Cardiff, 1952), p. 121, erroneously gives 1290 for his capture. The drawing before the hanging is mentioned by the so-called Wroxham Continuator: *Le livere des Reis de Brittanie*, ed. J. Glover (1865), p. 311. *Chronicon de Lanercost, 1201–1346*, ed. J. Stevenson (Bannatyne Club and Maitland Club, 1839), p. 145, for the statement that Rhys was left hanging for three days.

Chapter 8. The Lord

Page

86 The abbreviated copy of Domesday Book produced for William de Briouze is PRO E 164/1; Elizabeth Hallam, *Domesday Book through Nine Centuries* (London, 1986), photograph opposite p. 47, shows the annotation "Br'."

86–87 Washington and Findon in 1086: *Domesday Book: Sussex*, ed. and trans. John Morris (Chichester, 1976), nos. 13. 9, 11 (fol. 28).

88 The fortunes of William de Briouze senior as a minor can be traced through the Close and Patent Rolls.

88 The bare bones of the public career of William de Briouze senior can be found in *Parliamentary Writs*, ed. Francis Palgrave, 2 vols. in 4, Record Commission (1827–34), 1:495; *Knights of Edward I*, ed. C. Moor, 5 vols., Harleian Society 80–84 (1929–32), 1:144–45.

88–89 For William de Briouze's activities in 1264–65 see the Continuation of Gervase of Canterbury's *Gesta Regum*, ed. William Stubbs, *The Historical Works of Gervase of Canterbury*, 2 vols., RS (1879–80), 2:222, 235; *Annales Londonienses*, ed. William Stubbs, *Chronicles of the Reigns of Edward I and Edward II*, 2 vols., RS (1882–83), 1:62, and for his son as a hostage Charles Bémont, *Simon de Montfort* (Paris, 1884), pp. 353–55; *Manners and Household Expenses of England in the Thirteenth and Fifteenth Centuries*, ed. T. H. Turner, Roxburghe Club (1841), pp. 9, 10, 65, 66.

89 *Calendar of the Patent Rolls 1281–1292*, p. 230, for the trip overseas in 1286.

89 The basic facts of the public career of William de Briouze junior can be found in *Parliamentary Writs*, ed. Francis Palgrave, 2 vols. in 4, Record Commission (1827–34), 1:495–96; 2:589–91; *Knights of Edward I*, ed. C. Moor, 5 vols., Harleian Society 80–84 (1929–32), 1:145.

89 Marriage of Alina de Briouze and John de Mowbray: "Chronicle of the Thirteenth Century," *Archaeologia Cambrensis* 3rd ser. 8 (1862), pp. 272–83, at p. 283; *Cartae* 3, no. 758, p. 861.

89–90 For William de Briouze's outburst against Roger de Higham see *Select Cases in the Court of King's Bench* 3, ed. G. O. Sayles, Selden Society 58 (1939), no. 81, pp. 152–54; *Annales Londonienses*, ed. William Stubbs, *Chronicles of the Reigns of Edward I and Edward II*, 2 vols., RS (1882–83) 1:1–251, at p. 143.

90–91 On Marcher lordship in general see A. J. Otway-Ruthven, "The Constitutional Position of the Great Lordships in South Wales," *Transactions of the Royal Historical Society* 5th ser., 8 (1958), pp. 1–20; Rees Davies, *Lordship and Society in the March of Wales 1282–1400* (Oxford, 1978); idem, "Kings, Lords and Liberties in the March of Wales, 1066–1272," ibid. 5th ser., 29 (1979), pp. 41–61.

91 On Walter Clifford forcing the royal messenger to eat his letters see Matthew Paris, *Chronica majora*, ed. Henry R. Luard, 7 vols., RS (1872–84), 5:95.

91 The case of 1281 between William de Briouze and the earl of Gloucester: *Select Cases in the Court of King's Bench* 2, ed. G. O. Sayles, Selden Society 57 (1938), pp. lvii–lviii; *Cartae* 3, no. 741, pp. 810–11; Michael Altschul, *A Baronial Family in Medieval England: The Clares, 1217–1314* (Baltimore, 1965), p. 270.

91 On the inquests of 1274–75 and the quo warranto proceedings, see Donald W. Sutherland, *Quo Warranto Proceedings in the Reign of Edward I, 1278–1294* (Oxford, 1963).

92 For William de Briouze's rights in Bramber, see *Rotuli Hundredorum*, 2 vols., Record Commission (London, 1812–18), 2:201–3, trans. L. F. Salzmann, "The Hundred Roll for Sussex, Part 1," *Sussex Archaeological Collections* 82 (1942 for 1941): 20–34; *Placita de Quo Warranto*, Record Commission (London, 1818), p. 760.

93 For the dispute over the status of Gower see, in general, William Rees, "Gower and the March of Wales," *Archaeologia Cambrensis*

110 (1961): 1–29; *Glamorgan County History 3: The Middle Ages*, ed.
T. B. Pugh (Cardiff, 1971), pp. 231–43.

94 Bishop of Llandaff's status: *Calendar of the Patent Rolls 1292–1301*, p.
464; *Rot. Parl.* 1:42–43.

94 "primary jurisdiction": *Rot. Parl.* 1:143.

94 Philip IV's claim to *cognitio ordinaria* in Gascony cited by Maurice
Powicke, *The Thirteenth Century*, rev. ed. (Oxford, 1962), p. 645.

94 Parliamentary proceedings in 1300–1302 about Gower: *Rot. Parl.* 1:
143, 148–50.

95 King's grant of 1304: *Calendar of Charter Rolls 1300–1326*, pp. 46–47.

96 The record of the sessions of February 1306 is PRO JUST 1/1150; the
charters William issued are printed in *Charters Granted to
Swansea*, ed. George Grant Francis (London, 1867), pp. 5–19, with
translation, and photograph opposite p. 5, and *Cartae* 3, no. 851,
pp. 990–99; reference to the *magna carta de libertatibus Gouerhie*
ibid. 4, no. 958, p. 1191 (1334) (the original is BL Add. Ch. 1252).

Chapter 9. The Lady

Page

97 Weaverthorpe ("Werthorp"): *Calendar of Inquisitions Post Mortem* 6:
p. 459.

97 For summary details about the de Ros family see Ivor J. Sanders,
English Baronies (Oxford, 1961), p. 53.

98 Alina, first wife of William de Briouze senior, is mentioned in one
of his charters in 1254: Oxford, Magdalene College, Sele Charters,
Crokehurst Sussex 3; *The Chartulary of the Priory of St. Peter at
Sele*, ed. L. F. Salzman (Cambridge, 1923), no. 6, pp. 5–6. She
received the manor of Thorganby in Yorkshire as her *maritagium*
("dowry") from Thomas of Multon of Gilsland (d. 1271), presumably her father; Maud, widow of Thomas, recovered the manor
as her inheritance in 1281: PRO JUST 1/1050, m. 59 (corr. from
60); JUST 1/1055, mm. 23, 40, 57; CP 40/55, m. 19; *Calendar of
Inquisitions Miscellaneous* 1, no. 1244, p. 366.

98 The marriage of William de Briouze senior with the daughter of
Nicholas de Moeles: PRO JUST 1/1150, m. 2d. For Nicholas's
position: *Calendar of the Patent Rolls 1232–1247*, p. 459. The son,
Giles, who died in 1305, held a manor in Dorset given to his father
as a marriage portion by Nicholas de Moeles: *Calendar of Inquisitions Post Mortem* 6:168–69.

98 Provision for Richard, son of William and Mary de Briouze: *Select Cases in the Court of King's Bench* 4, ed. G. O. Sayles, Selden Society 74 (1955), no. 3, pp. 7–15.

99 *Calendar of the Close Rolls 1288–1296*, p. 196, for Lady Mary's dower of 1291.

99 The valuation of Lady Mary's Sussex estates is in PRO C143/119/8 (1316).

99 Edward I at Findon in 1305: *Calendar of the Patent Rolls 1301–1307*, p. 367; *Calendar of Inquisitions Miscellaneous* 1:534, for the writ issued there.

99 Valuation of Findon in 1291: *Taxatio ecclesiastica*, Record Commission (London, 1802), p. 134.

100 Litigation between Lady Mary and William de Briouze in 1292: *Rot. Parl.* 1:87–89.

100–101 Fine of 800 marks and dispute regarding Exchequer writs, 1293: *List of Welsh Entries in the Memoranda Rolls 1282–1343*, ed. Natalie Fryde (Cardiff, 1974), p. 8.

101 Richard and Peter de Briouze in 1295: *Book of Prests of the King's Wardrobe for 1294–1295: presented to John Goronwy Edwards*, ed. E. B. Fryde (Oxford, 1962), pp. 31, 165, 169–70, 172, 175, 202.

101 The case between Lady Mary, and Ralph de Camoys and his wife Margaret, in 1307: BL Add. Ch. 20036.

104 Pecham's letter to queen Eleanor is in John Pecham, *Registrum epistolarum*, ed. C. T. Martin, 3 vols., RS (1882–86) 2:555, no. 429; the biblical reference is Eccl. 36:27.

104 Eleanor "widely notorious for her land hunger": John Carmi Parsons, *Eleanor of Castile: Queen and Society in Thirteenth-Century England* (Basingstoke, 1994), p. 61.

Chapter 10. Narrative, Memory, and Inquisition
Page

106–7 On notaries in England see C. R. Cheney, *Notaries Public in England in the Thirteenth and Fourteenth Centuries* (Oxford, 1972).

106–7 Introduction and numbers of notaries: Cheney, *Notaries Public*, p. 33.

106–7 Adam of Lindsey: Cheney, *Notaries Public*, p. 84.

112 Sunehild of Swansea: PRO JUST 1/1150, mm. 2, 6.

114 Earl of Warwick's claim to Gower in 1278: *Cartae* 3, no. 740, pp. 805–8.

Chapter 11. The New Saint

Page

117 "when God first showed to the world": *Annales Prioratus de Wigornia*, ed. H. R. Luard, *Annales Monastici* 4, RS (1869), p. 493.

118 "inquiries should be made by the dean": *Registrum Ricardi de Swinfield 1283–1317*, ed. W. W. Capes, Cantilupe Society and Canterbury and York Soc. 6 (1909), p. 68.

118 Offerings at the shrine and dispute over wax tapers: Hereford Cathedral Archives 2368, 1418, the latter printed in *Charters and Records of Hereford Cathedral*, ed. W. W. Capes (Hereford, 1908), p. 167.

118 De Briouze family members mentioned in the Hereford obit book: Oxford, Bodleian Library, MS Rawlinson B 328, fols. 4v, 30, 30v.

118 Hugh de Briouze's illegitimacy is mentioned in *Calendar of Entries in the Papal Register relating to Great Britain and Ireland* 2, p. 27.

118–19 Letter of Bishop Swinfield of 19 April 1290: *Registrum Ricardi de Swinfield*, pp. 234–35, here misdated.

119 Letter of Bishop Sutton, 1294: *The Rolls and Register of Bishop Oliver Sutton* 5, ed. R.M.T. Hill, Lincoln Record Society 60 (1965), p. 32.

119 Dispute between canons and their representative at the papal court: Hereford Cathedral Archives 1419, printed in *Charters and Records of Hereford Cathedral*, ed. W. W. Capes (Hereford, 1908), pp. 162–63.

120 Edward I's letter: *Foedera, conventiones, litterae et . . . acta publica . . .*, ed. Thomas Rymer, new ed., 4 vols. in 7 parts, Record Commission (1816–69), 1/ii:985; *Calendar of the Close Rolls 1302–1307*, p. 436.

120 Receipt for £20 for expenses of William de Testa and acknowledgment for £3 paid out to a notary: Hereford Cathedral Archives 1439, 2673.

120–21 The report on the cardinals' investigations in 1313 is in MS Vatican City, Biblioteca Apostolica Vaticana, Ottob. Lat. 2516; the inventory of documents is on fols. 44v–45v.

122 The anonymous analyst on the case of Roger of Conway: André Vauchez, *Sainthood in the Late Middle Ages*, Eng. trans. (Cambridge, 1997), p. 547.

122–23 The account of the canonization of 1320 is in Berhard Schimmelpfennig, *Die Zeremonienbücher der römischen Kurie im Mittel-*

alter (Tübingen, 1973), pp. 164–66; the canonization bull itself is in *Acta sanctorum*, Octobris 1, pp. 596–98.

Chapter 12. Aftermath

Page

126 For general information on Durand see the note on p. 145.

126 On the trial of the Templars see Malcolm Barber, *The Trial of the Templars* (Cambridge, 1978); the records of the inquiry in which William Durand participated are printed in *Procès des Templiers*, ed. J. Michelet, 2 vols., Collection de documents inédits sur l'histoire de France (1841–51), 1.

128 For 205 as the number of witnesses in the Cantilupe canonization process see Ronald C. Finucane, *Miracles and Pilgrims: Popular Beliefs in Medieval England* (London, 1977), pp. 176–77, and the list in Michael Richter, *Sprache und Gesellschaft im Mittelalter* (Stuttgart, 1979), pp. 205–17. Other scholars have come to different conclusions, e. g. Patrick Daly in Meryl Jancey (ed.), *Saint Thomas Cantilupe, Bishop of Hereford: Essays in His Honour* (Hereford, 1982), p. 131, who gives 181.

128 The paper volume recording the work of the papal commission into the Templars is now Paris, BN lat. 11796, and the parchment roll is in the Vatican: see K. Schottmüller, *Der Untergang des Templer-Orden* 2 (Berlin, 1887), pp. 420–22.

129 Pope Clement's invitation and Durand on the need for reform: William Durand, *Tractatus de modo generalis concilii celebrandi* (Lyons, 1531), fol. 4; Constantine Fasolt was kind enough to provide a complete photocopy of the text.

129 The remarks of John XXII on Durand in his *Lettres secrètes*, ed. A. Coulon and S. Clemencet (Paris, 1906), nos. 849–50 (1319).

129–30 For William Durand on the need to speak the local language see *Tractatus de modo generalis concilii celebrandi* (Lyons, 1531) 2. 15, fols. 22–22v; for his promotion of his cousin William Carrerie, and of his relatives in general, see Constantine Fasolt, *Council and Hierarchy: The Political Thought of William Durant the Younger* (Cambridge, 1991), pp. 98–99 n. 83.

130 Durand's trip in 1320: *Foedera, conventiones, litterae et . . . acta publica . . .*, ed. Thomas Rymer, new ed., 4 vols. in 7 parts, Record Commission (1816–69), 2/i:431; as mediator between England and Scotland in 1321: ibid., pp. 442, 450; *Annales Paulini*, ed. William

Stubbs, *Chronicles of the Reigns of Edward I and Edward II*, 2 vols., RS (1882–83) 1:255–370, at p. 291.

130–31 William Durand's crusade treatise is printed in Gottfried Dürr-holder, *Die Kreuzzugspolitik unter Papst Johann XXII (1316–1334)* (Strassburg, 1913), pp. 103–10; Michael Foster was good enough to procure a copy of this.

132 On the trial of the Templars in England see Barber, *Trial*, pp. 193–204. The phrase "abominable and hateful things said" in Edward II's letter: *Foedera*, ed. Rymer, p. 10; the order for the arrest: *Calendar of the Close Rolls 1307–1313*, pp. 14, 48–49.

132 The sheriff of Carmarthen claimed his expenses and those of his posse when taking Llanmadoc into the king's hands: PRO SC6/1202/3.

132 *Concilia Magnae Britanniae*, ed. David Wilkins, 4 vols. (London, 1737) 2:329–64, 383–88, has a summary of proceedings against the Templars in London from MS Bodleian 454.

133 Appointment of the Ordainers: *Vita Edwardi Secundi*, ed. N. Denholm-Young (London, 1957), p. 9.

133–34 Bishop Baldock's letter to Saint Osyth's: *Registrum Radulphi Baldock, Gilberti Segrave, Ricardi Newport et Stephani Gravesend, episcoporum Londoniensium, 1304–1338*, ed. R. C. Fowler, Canterbury and York Soc. 7 (1911), p. 148.

133–34 The evidence about Roger of Conway is in Vat. Lat. 4015, fols. 188–203v; *Acta sanctorum*, Octobris I, pp. 626–28, 630–31; Oxford, Exeter Coll. MS 158, fols. 38v–39. This was one of the cases that the anonymous papal analyst discussed (see above, chapter II).

134–35 *Registrum Radulphi Baldock*, p. 73, on wrestling in Barking; *Calendar of the Close Rolls 1307–1313*, pp. 116–17, on the right of bishops of London to stranded whales.

134 For bishop Baldock's books and bequests see A. B. Emden, *A Biographical Register of the University of Oxford to A.D. 1500*, 3 vols. (Oxford, 1957–59) 3:2147–49; Historical Manuscripts Commission, *Ninth Report* and appendix, pt. 1, Dean and Chapter of Saint Pauls (London), p. 46.

135 For general information on Testa see the note on p. 145.

135 The Riccardi case: *Regestum Clementis Papae V* (Rome, 1885–92), nos. 2294–96.

136–37 William de Testa's involvement in the canonization of Thomas Aquinas: *Fontes vitae sancti Thomae Aquinatis* 4, ed. M. H. Laurent, *Revue thomiste* (1934), p. 270.

137 William de Testa's will is printed in François Duchesne, *Histoire de tous les cardinaux françois: Preuves* (Paris, 1660), pp. 279–83.

138 The litigation involving Thomas de Briouze in the 1330s: *Select Cases in the Court of King's Bench* 4, ed. G. O. Sayles, Selden Society 74 (1955), p. xliv.

138 For the chapel block at Oystermouth see *An Inventory of the Ancient Monuments in Glamorgan 3: Medieval Secular Monuments: Part 1b, the Later Castles* (Aberystwyth, 2000), pp. 266–71.

138 William, son of William de Briouze junior, is mentioned in 1306, 1311, and 1315: BL Harl. 152, fol. 11; PRO C71/4, m. 4; *Cartae* 3, nos. 865–66, 869–70, pp. 1021–23, 1026–28.

138 For the political crisis of 1320 see J. Conway Davies, "The Despenser War in Glamorgan," *Transactions of the Royal Historical Society*, 3rd ser., 9 (1915): 21–64.

139 William de Briouze junior "very rich by descent": Thomas Walsingham, *Historia Anglicana*, ed. H. T. Riley, 2 vols., RS (1863–64) 1:158.

139 William's debts in the 1280s: *Calendar of the Close Rolls 1279–1288*, pp. 237, 356, 357; negotiations over Wickhambreux: *Literae Cantuarienses*. ed. J. B. Sheppard, 3 vols., RS (1887–89) 1:104–7.

139 "offering it for sale to many lords": John of Trokelowe, *Annales*, ed. H. T. Riley, 2 vols., RS (1866), p. 107.

140 On the execution of John de Mowbray in 1322: *Gesta Edwardi de Carnarvan auctore canonico Bridlingtoniensi*, ed. William Stubbs, in *Chronicles of the Reigns of Edward I and Edward II*, 2 vols., RS (1882–83), 2:23–151, at p. 78; "A Chronicle of the Civil Wars of Edward II," ed. George L. Haskins, *Speculum* 14 (1939): 73–81, at p. 79.

141 Surveys of the estates of William and Mary de Briouze at their deaths: *Calendar of Inquisitions Post Mortem* 6:435–36, 458–59.

Index

Medieval people are indexed under first name.